Elizabethan England

Titles in the World History Series

Elizabethan England

by
William W. Lace

Lucent Books, P.O. Box 289011, San Diego, CA 92198-9011

Library of Congress Cataloging-in-Publication Data

Lace, William W.
    Elizabethan England / by William W. Lace
        p. cm.—(World history series)
    Includes bibliographical references and index.
    ISBN 1-56006-278-9 (alk. paper)
    1. Great Britain—History—Elizabeth, 1558-1603—Juvenile
literature. 2. England—Civilization—16th century—Juvenile literature. [1. Great Britain—History—Elizabeth, 1558-1603.
2. England—Civilization.] I.Title. II. Series.
DA355.L33   1995
942.05'5—dc20   94-11569
                                                           CIP
                                                           AC

Copyright 1995 by Lucent Books, Inc., P.O. Box 289011,
San Diego, California, 92198-9011

Printed in the U.S.A.

Contents

Foreword

Each year on the first day of school, nearly every history teacher faces the task of explaining why his or her students should study history. One logical answer to this question is that exploring what happened in our past explains how the things we often take for granted—our customs, ideas, and institutions—came to be. As statesman and historian Winston Churchill put it, "Every nation or group of nations has its own tale to tell. Knowledge of the trials and struggles is necessary to all who would comprehend the problems, perils, challenges, and opportunities which confront us today." Thus, a study of history puts modern ideas and institutions in perspective. For example, though the founders of the United States were talented and creative thinkers, they clearly did not invent the concept of democracy. Instead, they adapted some democratic ideas that had originated in ancient Greece and with which the Romans, the British, and others had experimented. An exploration of these cultures, then, reveals their very real connection to us through institutions that continue to shape our daily lives.

Another reason often given for studying history is the idea that lessons exist in the past from which contemporary societies can benefit and learn. This idea, although controversial, has always been an intriguing one for historians. Those that agree that society can benefit from the past often quote philosopher George Santayana's famous statement, "Those who cannot remember the past are condemned to repeat it." Historians who ascribe to Santayana's philosophy believe that, for example, studying the events that led up to the major world wars or other significant historical events would allow society to chart a different and more favorable course in the future.

Just as difficult as convincing students to realize the importance of studying history is the search for useful and interesting supplementary materials that present historical events in a context that can be easily understood. The volumes in Lucent Books' World History Series attempt to present a broad, balanced, and penetrating view of the march of history. Ancient Egypt's important wars and rulers, for example, are presented against the rich and colorful backdrop of Egyptian religious, social, and cultural developments. The series engages the reader by enhancing historical events with these cultural contexts. For example, in *Ancient Greece*, the text covers the role of women in that society. Slavery is discussed in *The Roman Empire*, as well as how slaves earned their freedom. The numerous and varied aspects of everyday life in these and other societies are explored in each volume of the series. Additionally, the series covers the major political, cultural, and philosophical ideas as the torch of civilization is passed from ancient Mesopotamia and Egypt, through Greece, Rome, Medieval Europe, and other world cultures, to the modern day.

The material in the series is formatted in a thorough, precise, and organized manner. Each volume offers the reader a comprehensive and clearly written overview of an important historical event or period. The topic under discussion is placed in a broad, historical context. For example, *The Italian Renaissance* begins with a discussion of the High Middle Ages and the loss of central control that allowed certain Italian cities to develop artistically. The book ends by looking forward to the Reformation and interpreting the societal changes that grew out of the Renaissance. Thus, students are not only involved in an historical era, but also enveloped by the events leading up to that era and the events following it.

One important and unique feature in the World History Series is the primary and secondary source quotations that richly supplement each volume. These quotes are useful in a number of ways. First, they allow students access to sources they would not normally be exposed to because of the difficulty and obscurity of the original source. The quotations range from interesting anecdotes to far-sighted cultural perspectives and are drawn from historical witnesses both past and present. Second, the quotes demonstrate how and where historians themselves derive their information on the past as they strive to reach a consensus on historical events. Lastly, all of the quotes are footnoted, familiarizing students with the citation process and allowing them to verify quotes and/or look up the original source if the quote piques their interest.

Finally, the books in the World History Series provide a detailed launching point for further research. Each book contains a bibliography specifically geared toward student research. A second, annotated bibliography introduces students to all the sources the author consulted when compiling the book. A chronology of important dates gives students an overview, at a glance, of the topic covered. Where applicable, a glossary of terms is included.

In short, the series is designed not only to acquaint readers with the basics of history, but also to make them aware that their lives are a part of an ongoing human saga. Perhaps they will then come to the same realization as famed historian Arnold Toynbee. In his monumental work, *A Study of History,* he wrote about becoming aware of history flowing through him in a mighty current, and of his own life "welling like a wave in the flow of this vast tide."

Important Dates in the History of Elizabethan England

1533	1535	1540	1545	1550	1555	1560	156

1533
Elizabeth I is born (September 7).

1536
Elizabeth's mother, Anne Boleyn, is executed.

1540
Founding of Royal College of Surgeons; beginning of surgery as a profession.

1547
Henry VIII dies; Elizabeth's younger brother, Edward VI, becomes King of England.

1553
Edward VI dies; Elizabeth's older sister, Mary I, becomes Queen of England; Hugh Willoughby and Richard Chancellor fail to find Northwest Passage to Asia but open trade with Russia.

1554
Elizabeth imprisoned in Tower of London but cannot be proved guilty of treason.

1557
Thomas Tusser writes the *Hundred Points of Good Husbandry*, the first popular book on agriculture.

1558
Mary I dies; Elizabeth I becomes Queen of England.

1559
Elizabeth's coronation (January 15); religious Acts of Settlement enacted by Parliament.

1560
Amy, wife of Robert Dudley, Earl of Leicester, found dead; death ruled a suicide.

1561
Mary Queen of Scots returns to Scotland from France.

1562
John Hawkins begins slave trade with Spanish in the New World.

1564
Births of William Shakespeare and Christopher Marlowe.

1565
Mary Queen of Scots marries Lord Darnley.

1566
Birth of Mary Queen of Scots' son, James, future King of England.

1567
English colonization of North America suggested by Sir Humphrey Gilbert; Royal Exchange built in London.

1568
Hawkins's fleet attacked by Spain at San Juan de Ulloa, thus beginning hostilities between Spain and England; Mary Queen of Scots flees Scotland, takes refuge in England, and is made a virtual prisoner.

1570
Elizabeth excommunicated from Catholic church by Pope Pius V.

1571
First of Sir Francis Drake's voyages to Spanish possessions in the New World.

1572
A new star appears, upsetting established beliefs about the unchangeability of the heavens.

1576
English mathematician Thomas Digges suggests stars are actually other suns; The Theatre built in London by James Burbage.

1577
Drake embarks for voyage around the world.

1580
Jesuit priests sent to England by Catholic church.

1582
Gilbert founds first English colony in America in Newfoundland.

1584
Sir Walter Raleigh receives authorization from Elizabeth to colonize the New World.

1585
First colony at Roanoke, Virginia, established.

1587
Execution of Mary Queen of Scots; Francis Drake raids Spanish fleet at Cadiz; *Tamburlaine* establishes Marlowe as leading playwright.

1588
Defeat of Spanish Armada by English navy; death of Robert Dudley, Earl of Leicester.

1590
Roanoke colony found abandoned, temporarily halting English attempts to colonize North America.

1592
Shakespeare's first plays, the three-part *Henry VI*, performed.

1593
Marlowe killed.

1594
Lord Chamberlain's Players, the most famous of Elizabethan acting companies, founded; Shakespeare's *Love's Labour's Lost* and *Romeo and Juliet* performed.

1598
Death of Elizabeth's closest adviser, William Cecil, Lord Burghley.

1599
Globe theater opens with Shakespeare's *Henry V*.

1600
Dr. William Gilbert publishes *De Magnete*, opening way for study of electronics; Shakespeare's *Julius Caesar* performed.

1601
Elizabeth speaks to Parliament for last time; Shakespeare's *Hamlet* performed.

1603
Death of Elizabeth (March 24).

The English Renaissance

On November 17, 1558, Queen Mary I, the second of King Henry VIII's children to rule England, died. Instead of sorrow, however, her death touched off celebration. People danced around bonfires in London. Only days earlier, other fires had consumed the bodies of six men condemned by Mary to burn at the stake for their religious beliefs.

Mary's reign had been a national nightmare—defeat in warfare abroad, religious strife at home. England's wealth had been swallowed by war, and her spirit had been exhausted in the bitter struggle between Roman Catholics and Protestants, those who sought to free the church from Rome and the popes.

Now, the English, except for the Catholic minority, celebrated what they hoped would be a new age of peace, freedom, and prosperity. They rested these hopes on a twenty-five-year-old girl—Elizabeth Tudor, Mary's younger sister and the last living child of Henry VIII. A week later, as Elizabeth rode toward London, the people went out to meet her, "with so lively representations of love, joy, and hope that it far exceeded her expectations."[1]

Elizabeth's reign was to exceed their wildest dreams. She would rule for forty-five years over what would forever be known as the Elizabethan Age. England

Elizabeth on her way to her coronation. Elizabeth's reign would usher in the Renaissance in England.

would become a respected power in Europe: She would expand overseas. Her people would become wealthy. The arts would flourish. Law and government would continue to develop toward a form that eventually would spread throughout the world.

Long after Elizabeth's death, her reign would be remembered as England's golden age. Indeed, November 17 was celebrated as a national holiday for almost two hundred years. Even while she ruled, her subjects knew they were living in a special time. They called her "Gloriana" because of the glory she had brought to the country. A song of the period said:

> But whereto shall we bend our lays
>   [songs]?
> Even up to Heaven, again to raise

The Maid which, thence descended,
Hath brought again the golden days
And all the world amended.[2]

A Late Blooming

The Elizabethan Age represented the English flowering of the Renaissance, or "rebirth," of learning and culture that had begun in Italy around 1400. In these times, journeys between countries were measured in weeks or months, but ideas traveled even

People celebrate May Day at the time of Elizabeth. Under Elizabeth's rule, the arts flourished, wealth grew, and England's influence abroad expanded.

more slowly. The seeds of Renaissance Italy went far and wide. Some countries provided more fertile ground than others.

Certainly, the Renaissance was slow taking root in England. First, the bloody civil conflict known as the Wars of the Roses desolated the country. Then, after a brief blooming of the arts under Henry VIII, religious strife divided the people. Only the extended peace brought by Elizabeth allowed true English culture, not a copy of the Italian, to develop. As historian A. L. Rowse wrote, "It took the best part of a century to catch up."[3]

Elizabeth cannot be given full credit for the accomplishments of Elizabethan England. She was careful, cautious, and conservative. Some achievements during her reign occurred despite her wishes, not because of them. Rather, it was her personality—joyous, confident, and defiant—that served as an example to her people and gave them a patriotism never felt before. The people loved Elizabeth, and that love inspired them. Historian A. H. Dodd wrote:

> The whole age is colored by the rich personality of the Queen herself, but never swamped by it: one of her triumphs was the active response she drew from a wide range of social levels and geographical areas, making her reign equally an age of the ordinary Englishmen. For what elicited [brought forth] the response was devotion not so much to the abstract concept of England as to a living person, seen through a haze of romance yet decidedly human and accessible.[4]

Chapter

1 Gloriana and Her Court

Other periods in history have been named after rulers, but none so completely revolved around the personality of the monarch as did the Elizabethan Age. It was a complex, turbulent time, and Elizabeth was a complex, turbulent person.

She could be cold and cruel. She would fly into rages, boxing the ears of one adviser and throwing her slipper in the face of another, but "when she smiled, it was a pure sunshine."[5] She was intelligent and well educated but also was fond of drinking beer, spitting, picking her teeth, and swearing "round, mouth-filling oaths."[6]

She would do almost anything to avoid making a difficult decision. When urged to do one thing or another by her counselors, she would most often do nothing. As she once wrote King Henri III of France, "I have let time pass, which I generally find helps more than reasoning."[7]

Constantly on display, she was nevertheless the most private of persons. She never confided completely in anyone. She had learned a hard lesson growing up during the reigns of her brother and sister— keep your thoughts to yourself and your mouth shut and you might keep your head on your shoulders. She once wrote:

I grieve; and dare not show my discontent!

I love; and yet am forced to seem to hate!
I do, yet dare not say, I ever meant! [8]

Elizabeth had a complex personality. She could be both elegant and crude, sensitive and cruel. But no era was more marked by a personality than the Elizabethan Era.

Philip II (left) with Mary I, was Elizabeth's first suitor. Although citizens of her time expected her to marry and produce an heir, Elizabeth avoided marriage and ruled her country alone.

The most immediate question when Elizabeth became queen was that of her marriage. The question was not *if* she would marry, but *when*. She was expected to produce an heir. Besides, the notion that a woman could rule by herself, without a strong husband, was unheard of.

Elizabeth's first suitor was her dead sister's husband Philip, now King of Spain, who wanted to maintain the alliance with England. She pretended to be flattered. She protested that she was not worthy. Actually, she had fallen in love with Robert Dudley, Earl of Leicester. Leicester, however, was already married.

A Royal Scandal

Many believed Elizabeth and Leicester were lovers. The scandal reached a climax when, in September 1560, Leicester's wife, Amy, was found dead at the bottom of a staircase, her neck broken. The official verdict in the death was suicide, but many people thought Leicester had his wife murdered. Elizabeth's rival, Mary Queen of Scots, said to the French court, "The Queen of England is going to marry her horse-keeper, who has killed his wife to make room for her."[9]

At first, Elizabeth ignored the gossip. Gradually, her most trusted councillor, William Cecil, Lord Burghley, convinced her that, even if she might gain a husband, she might lose her throne. Elizabeth came to her senses. She sent Leicester tem-

Mary Queen of Scots remained Elizabeth's main rival throughout her reign. She was next in line to inherit the throne if anything happened to Elizabeth.

porarily away from court. While he remained close to her throughout their long lives, there was no chance of marriage.

Actually, Elizabeth was afraid of marriage. Marriage had brought death to her mother, Anne Boleyn, and heartbreak and despair to her sister Mary. In addition, she had no wish to share any of her power with a husband. "God's death!" she once shouted at Leicester. "I will have here but one mistress and no master."[10] And when Parliament called on her to marry, she replied, "I am already bound to a husband, which is the kingdom of England."[11] The pressure on Elizabeth to marry was so intense because the person next in line for the throne would be a disastrous monarch for England. This was Mary Queen of Scots, a granddaughter of Henry VIII's sister Margaret, who had married King James IV of Scotland. While still an infant, Mary became Queen of Scotland, was engaged to be married to the eldest son of the King of France, and was sent to be raised in the French court. When she was seventeen, her husband, King Francis II, died. Mary

On Choosing a Wife

William Cecil, Lord Burghley, wrote long letters full of advice to his son, Robert. In this excerpt, found in Lacey Baldwin Smith, The Horizon Book of the Elizabethan World, *Burghley tells his idea of the ideal wife.*

"The next and greatest care ought to be in choice of a wife, and the only danger therein is beauty, by which all men in all ages, wise and foolish, have been betrayed. And although I know it vain to use reasons or arguments to dissuade thee from being captivated therewith, there being few or none that ever resisted that witchery, yet I cannot omit to warn thee as of other things which may be thy ruin and destruction. For the present time it is true that every man prefers his fantasy in that appetite before all other worldly desires, leaving the care of honor, credit, and safety in respect thereof. But remember that though these affections do not last, yet the bond of marriage dureth [lasts] to the end of thy life; and therefore better to be borne withal in a mistress than in a wife, for when thy humor shall change thou art yet free to choose again (if thou give thyself that vain liberty). Remember, secondly, that if thou marry for beauty thou bindest thyself for all thy life for that which perchance will neither last nor please thee one year; and when thou hast it, it will be unto thee of no price at all, for the desire dieth when it is attained and the affection perisheth when it is satisfied."

returned to Scotland in 1561 to take up her duties as queen.

Elizabeth would always have plenty of eligible suitors eager to marry her. Most were not taken seriously, and Elizabeth kept them dangling—partially because of politics and partially because it gave her pleasure to be wooed. She was extraordinarily vain and in love with being loved. It was little wonder that everything—government, culture, religion, society—revolved around the queen, much like planets circling the sun. Those closest to the center of power and who shone brightly in its glow made up Elizabeth's court.

The court was like a magnet, attracting the best and worst of society. The most talented musicians, the most gifted playwrights, the most able administrators, the most dashing men, and the most beautiful women vied with one another for places close to Elizabeth. Yet, because court was the origin of all wealth and power, it was also a place where treachery, jealousy, and scandal abounded. A poet of the time, Anthony Munday, wrote:

> My first day's walk was to the court,
> Where beauty fed mine eyes:
> Yet found I that the courtly sport
> Did mask in sly disguise.
> For falsehoods sat in fairest looks
> And friend to friend was coy;
> Court favor fill'd but empty books
> And there I found no joy.[12]

A Court on the Move

The court was wherever Elizabeth happened to be. She had many royal residences —Hampton Court, Whitehall, Nonsuch,

Elizabeth and her entourage enter London. In her time, a queen was expected to travel frequently among the people.

and Greenwich, among others—and moved among them throughout the year. These changes were made because of the lack of sanitation at the time. Although water was piped into these palaces for drinking, washing, and cooking, there was no plumbing for toilets. Ladies and gentlemen used "close stools" (portable wooden toilets), and servants used outdoor privies. Floors were covered with straw and quickly became foul with food scraps and animal droppings. When one palace became uninhabitable, the court moved on to another.

Court was where ambitious sons and daughters of noble families came from throughout the kingdom to seek their fortunes. For men, the first step was to get a permanent, salaried place in court as part

Intrigue at Court

Elizabeth's court was a place where the greatest men in the kingdom vied with one another for the attention and favor of the queen. When she showed favor to one courtier, it was bound to create jealousy in another, as this excerpt from a letter by the Earl of Essex shows. It is found in The Horizon Book of the Elizabethan World.

"Yesternight the queen came to Worth Hall. . . . She came to speak of [Sir Walter] Raleigh, and it seemed she could not well endure any thing to be spoken against him; and taking hold of one word, 'disdain,' she said there was no such cause why I should disdain him. This speech troubled me so much that as near as I could I described unto her what he had been and what he was, and then I did let her see whether I had cause to disdain his competition of love, or whether I could have comfort to give myself over to the service of a mistress that was in awe of such a man. I spake, what of grief and choler, as much against him as I could, and I think he standing at the door might very well hear the worse that I spoke of himself. In the end I saw she was resolved to defend him, and to cross me. . . . I told her . . . I had no joy to be in any place but loathe to be near about her when I knew my affection so much thrown down, and such a wretch as Raleigh highly esteemed of her. To this she made no answer, but turned away to my lady of Warwick. This strange alteration is by Raleigh's means, and the queen that hath tried all other ways now will see whether she can by these hard courses drive me to be friends with Raleigh, which rather shall drive me to many other extremities."

Elizabeth receives an ambassador at court. Knowing the queen's weakness for flattery, men vied for her attention in the hopes of receiving a position.

Hampton Court palace was just one of the queen's many residences. Having several residences was not a result of vanity, but necessity—poor sanitation made a residence unlivable after a few months.

of the queen's household or that of one of the chief ministers. They would try to catch the eye of a Burghley or a Leicester who might give them a position or who, in turn, might bring them to the attention of the queen, who might appoint them to an office. These offices—"Clerk of the Wardrobe," for instance—sounded humble but were considered positions of honor and were held by members of the upper classes. The actual work was done by servants.

Only men were named to such offices. Young women came to court hoping to find a place among the queen's many maids of honor. If a maid of honor served Elizabeth faithfully, she could look forward to a wealthy arranged marriage. She risked losing everything, however, if she married without the queen's permission or—worse yet—became pregnant out of wedlock.

Elizabeth Throckmorton was one of the fortunate maids of honor. Her brother went to considerable trouble and expense to obtain a position for her close to the queen. She served well and wound up marrying Sir Walter Raleigh, one of the queen's favorites. Not as lucky was Mary Fitton. In 1601, Robert Cecil wrote about

a misfortune befallen Mistress Fitton, for she is proved with child, and the Earl of Pembroke, being examined, confesseth a fact, but utterly renounceth all marriage. I fear they will both dwell in the

Tower awhile, for the Queen had vowed to send them thither.[13]

Positions for Sale

Obtaining a place at court was not easy. There were many job seekers and few jobs. Only those from the most noble families could be assured of a position. Others had to buy their way in. To even get an interview, a newcomer often had to offer a gift, actually a bribe, to someone who could provide an introduction to the queen and her leading ministers. One father spent more than £1,300—enough to buy several good-sized farms—to make his daughter a maid of honor.

Physical attractiveness, elegant clothes, and polished manners were good ways to attract the attention of the powerful, and especially of Elizabeth. A hundred years earlier, a man's fighting ability was about the only thing needed for success. The ideal gentleman of Elizabeth's court was not only a fighter, but also a graceful dancer, a good singer, a poet, and—above all—a well-spoken flatterer.

Elizabeth never grew tired of hearing her beauty, wisdom, courage, or any other

Plotting by the Numbers

Secrecy and intrigue were everywhere in Elizabeth's court, with various factions plotting against one another. Sometimes, people wrote to one another in code to avoid detection in case their letters were intercepted. This letter from one Rowland White to Sir Robert Sidney, found in The Horizon Book of the Elizabethan World, *substituted numbers for names.*

"Nine thousand [Lord Herbert] is highly favored by 1500 [Queen Elizabeth] for at his departure he had access unto her and was private an hour; but he greatly wants advice and extremely longs for you here. This day he is gone to see 2000 [the Earl of Pembroke's father], but will be here again before Christmas. He bids me assure you privately that he will undertake to bring 2000 to resign over unto you presently, the place desired by you, if you found yourself strong in friends at 160 [the court] to compass it. . . . Nine any reward; that this being a voluntary resignation, if it be thousand is very well beloved here of all, especially by 200 [Sir Robert Cecil] and 40 [Sir Walter Raleigh], who protests in all places they love him. I have some cause to believe that 600 [the Earl of Nottingham] would desire to have him match in his house. I only answer that a fitter instrument than yourself cannot be found out, if you may be brought to deal in it, which peradventure you might do, if you were here."

Elizabeth and her procession. The queen and her entourage dressed elegantly mainly to impress one another.

virtue praised. She delighted in keeping suitors and admirers in constant attendance. As she grew older and tried to maintain a youthful appearance with wigs and makeup, the flattery grew more extreme. Elizabeth was nearly sixty years old when Raleigh wrote, in a letter Elizabeth was meant to see:

> My heart was never broken till this day that I hear the Queen goes away so far off. . . . I am now left behind her in a dark prison all alone . . . I that was wont to behold her riding like Alexander, hunting like Diana, walking like Venus, the gentle wind blowing her fair hair around her pure cheeks like a nymph, sometime sitting in the shade like a goddess, sometime singing like an angel, sometime playing like Orpheus.[14]

A Game Played Too Long

Elizabeth was a shameless flirt. She pretended to be angry but was secretly delighted when men came to blows or fought duels over her. It was all very charming when she was young, but later the court was marked by "an often coarse frivolity, by a false hilarity . . . or by the elaborate make-believe of flirtation which had to be kept up long after it had lost all point or savour. It was all frankly vulgar."[15] Even Raleigh became bitter and wrote, "Go tell the court it glows and shines like rotten wood."[16]

Outwardly, at least, the court was all glitter and gaiety. There was dancing nearly every night, and the queen joined in—almost until her death at the age of sixty-nine.

The most elaborate entertainments were the court masques, intricate dramas with musical accompaniment, often on classical Greek or Roman themes. Members of the court took part, wearing fantastic costumes and masks. Masques were conducted in huge "banqueting houses," pavilions up to four-hundred feet around and elegantly decorated. In 1572, a French ambassador wrote of a banqueting house "spangled with gold and richly hung" that had required five-hundred men to decorate.[17]

A successful courtier had to look the part. One of the most distinctive aspects of the Elizabethan Age was the extreme, sometimes bizarre, manner of dress. A seventeenth-century historian, William Camden, wrote:

In these days a wondrous excess of apparel had spread itself all over England [which] grew into such contempt, that men by their new fangled garments, and too gaudy apparel, discovered a certain deformity and arrogancy of mind whilst they jetted up and down in their silks glittering with gold and silver, either embroidered or laced.[18]

The Ruff

The distinctive feature of Elizabethan fashion was the ruff, a construction of starched material that stuck out in a circle from around the neck and was held in place with hundreds of sticks. Ruffs were very fragile, and the wearer had to avoid brush-

---

Noble Feasts

William Harrison's Description of England *included this description of the diet of the upper classes. Notice that French chefs already were in demand. The passage is found in* Elizabethan People: State and Society, *edited by Joel Hurstfield and Alan G. R. Smith.*

"In number of dishes and change of meat the nobility of England (whose cooks are for the most part musical-headed Frenchmen and strangers) do most exceed, since there is no day . . . that passeth over their heads, wherein they have not only beef, mutton, veal, lamb, kid, port, cony [rabbit], capon [a fowl], pig, or so many of these as the season yieldeth, but also some portion of the red or fallow deer, beside great variety of fish and wild fowl, and thereto sundry other delicates wherein the sweet hand of the seafaring Portingale [Portuguese] is not wanting: so that for a man to dine with one of them, and to taste of every dish that standeth before him, which few use to do . . . is rather to yield unto a conspiracy with a great deal of meat for the speedy suppression of natural health that the use of a necessary mean to satisfy himself with a competent repast to sustain his body withal."

Making a Goodly Show

Appearances were everything at Elizabeth's court, and it was not unusual for people to try to get attention by spending everything they had on clothes. William Harrison had this impression of court dress in his Description of England. *The passage is found in* The Horizon Book of the Elizabethan World *by Lacey Baldwin Smith.*

"How curious, how nice also, are a number of men and women, and how hardly can the tailor please them in making it fit for their bodies! How many times must it be sent back again to him that made it! What chafing, what fretting, what reproachful language doth the poor workman bear away! And many times when he doth nothing to it at all, yet when it is brought home again it is very fit and handsome; then must we put it on, then must the long seams of our hose be set by a plumb line; then we puff, then we blow, and finally sweat till we drop, that our clothes may stand well upon us. I will say nothing of our heads, which sometimes are polled, sometimes curled, or suffered to grow at length like woman's locks, many times cut off above or under the ears, round as by a wooden dish. Neither will I meddle with our variety of beards, of which some are shaven from the chin like those of Turks, not a few cut short like to the Beard of Marquess Otto, some made round like a rubbing brush, others with a pique devant [two points] (O fine fashion!) or now and then suffered to grow long, the barbers being grown to be so cunning in this behalf as the tailors. . . . Some lusty courtiers also and gentlemen of courage do wear either rings of gold, stones, or pearl in their ears, whereby they imagine the workmanship of God not to be a little amended. But herein they rather disgrace than adorn their persons, as by their niceness in apparel, for which I say most nations do not unjustly deride us, as also for that we . . . bestow most cost upon our arses, and much more than upon all the rest of our bodies, as women do likewise upon their heads and shoulders."

ing against walls, curtains, other people's ruffs, and—for obvious reasons—candles.

All this, of course, was very expensive. People hoping to make an impression at court frequently spent everything they had on a single outfit and thus "carry their whole estates upon their backs."[19] The most elaborate and costly apparel was that

Actors perform for their queen. Elizabeth was fond of the arts, and sponsored music, drama, art, and literature.

of Elizabeth. Every gown was covered with gold and silver braid, pearls, and jewels.

The Elizabethan court may have been gaudy and extravagant, but it also fostered much intellectual development. The best in music, art, drama, and literature was found at court. Foreign influence was considerable, with some of the most talented persons in France, Italy, and the Netherlands working in London. Their presence, in turn, influenced English writers and artists. The importance of Elizabeth's court, then, is not the glittering picture it presented, but the fact that it, as historian A. L. Rowse wrote, "was the effective point of contact with the Renaissance influences from abroad."[20]

2 London and the Towns

England in the Elizabethan Age was more peaceful and prosperous than it had been for more than a century. Trade flourished, and the centers of trade were the cities. The period featured a marked growth of cities, not only in size, but also in their importance.

In previous centuries, the large manor farms of the noblemen formed the center of the English economy. These farms were largely self-sufficient; almost everything the people needed was grown or made on the premises. Towns provided markets, places where people from the farms could bring goods to trade for what they could not produce.

The towns grew during the Tudor era because of changes in the economy. First, agriculture became more specialized. Farms grew the crops or raised the livestock best suited to the land instead of trying to produce a little of everything. This meant a great increase in the buying and selling of farm products among various parts of the country and thus a great increase in the size of market towns.

Second, the English economy under the Tudors began to shift from one dealing in raw materials to one manufacturing finished goods. The English were tired of paying high prices to other countries for goods that had been made from raw mate-

rials from England. Leather goods were made in Leicester using hides from surrounding cattle farms—hides that had previously been sold overseas. Instead of exporting raw wool, farmers around Norwich sold it to weavers in the town, who produced finished cloth. Instead of being

London became an important city during Elizabeth's reign. London merchants produced most of the goods needed throughout England.

shipped to Europe, iron ore went to cities like Sheffield, which soon became famous for its knives and tools. This manufacturing was centered in the towns and cities, thus increasing the population.

Rise of the Merchants

Manufacturing was done on a small scale—in households or small shops instead of in large factories, and a metalsmith in Sheffield, for instance, was not able to handle overseas sales himself. This function was performed by a merchant who would buy goods from several manufacturers and then arrange for their export and sale. The growth of trade in Elizabeth's reign and the movement toward a money economy (selling goods for cash instead of trading them for other goods) led to growth in the number and wealth of merchants. "Never in the annals of the modern world," wrote modern economist John Maynard Keynes, "has there existed so prolonged and so rich an opportunity for the business man."[21] It was the merchants, and the amount of wealth they controlled, who gave the cities economic power.

In Henry VIII's time, England had a total population of about 3 million, of which some 200,000 lived in towns and cities. By the end of Elizabeth's reign, the total population had climbed to 5 million and the number in cities to 1 million.

London was supreme in both size and influence. At the end of Elizabeth's reign, it was the largest city in northern Europe, with a population estimated at 300,000—seventeen times its nearest rival, Norwich.

A sixteenth-century London druggist plies his wares. Manufacturing during the Elizabethan Era was done on a small scale, shop by shop.

More than 90 percent of the country's overseas trade was done from London. London's importance, as a modern historian wrote, "surpassed that of all the rest of the leading towns together."[22]

Despite its population, London was nowhere near the sprawling metropolis it is today. Most of the people were crowded into and around the area bounded by the ancient city walls and the River Thames, containing the Tower of London and St. Paul's Cathedral. Open fields lay between London and Westminster, the center of government. Chelsea and other areas now considered the heart of the city were then simple country villages.

London was so powerful that it was governed almost independently of the

A Nation of Workers

"[People] are not suffered to be idle in their cities as they be in any other parts of Christendom, but every child of 6 or 7 years old is forced to some art whereby he gaineth his own living and something besides to help to enrich his parents or master. I have known in one city viz. [that is] Norwich where the accounts having been made yearly what children from 6 to 10 years have earned towards their keeping in a year, and it hath been accounted that it hath risen to 12,000 pounds sterling which they have gained, besides other keeping, and that chiefly by knitting of fine jersey stockings, every child being able at or soon after 7 years to earn four shillings a week at that trade, which the merchants uttered at London, and some trading therewith with France and other parts. And in that city I have known in my time 24 aldermen which were esteemed to be worth £20,000 a piece, some much more, and the better sort of citizens the half. But if we should speak of London and some other maritime places we should find it much exceeding this rate. It is well known that at this time there are in London some merchants worth £100,000, and he is not accounted rich that cannot reach to £50,000 or near it."

queen and her council. The merchants in London and the queen's ministers in Westminster were highly respectful of and needed one another. The royal government would have been hard-pressed to pay its bills without the taxes paid by the merchants. At the same time, the government passed laws—such as those placing taxes on imported goods—that guaranteed more profits for the merchants so that they could continue to pay taxes.

The Queen Helps London

Elizabeth was eager to please the London merchants. In 1580, for instance, the London council became concerned with the rapidly increasing population of the city's suburbs, over which they had no control. They asked Elizabeth to help them limit suburban growth. The queen accommodated them by proclaiming that no new houses should be built within three miles of the city unless there had previously been a house on the same spot.

London's most powerful forces were the twelve Livery Companies, groups of merchants that had evolved from the medieval guilds, craftsmen banded together to control their professions. There were companies for drapers, grocers, fishmongers, tailors, and mercers (textile dealers), among others. The city's governing council was made up of aldermen, one elected from each of London's twenty-four boroughs (sections). The aldermen, almost all members of the Livery Companies, selected the Lord Mayor. Even today, the City of London's aldermen must select the Lord Mayor from two candidates proposed by the Livery Companies.

The companies strictly controlled who would enter their respective professions, the standards of workmanship, and prices.

One could not sell fish, for instance, if he were not a member of the fishmongers company. One joined a company first as an apprentice, serving under a member of the company, and worked his way up to becoming a "freeman," a full member.

London was full of apprentices. They had left their families and lived with their masters. Although the masters sought to control their behavior, these young men were known for drinking and carousing.

A City of Filth

By today's standards, London was almost an unlivable city. The streets were crooked, narrow, and filthy. John Stow, who wrote a description of London at the time, said that one street, Chick Lane, was known by most people as "Stinking Lane." People simply dumped their garbage in the street

A view of London in 1584 shows that the city was crammed into a small area, with fields separating it from the seat of Elizabeth's government in Westminster.

Londoners

London was one of the largest and proudest cities in Europe during the Elizabethan Era. This description was left by Duke Frederick of Würtenberg after a visit in 1592. It is found in Elizabethan People: State and Society.

"[London] is a very populous city, so that one can scarcely pass along the streets, on account of the throng. The inhabitants are magnificently apparelled, and are extremely proud and overbearing; and because the greater part, especially the trades people, seldom go into other countries, but always remain in their houses in the city attending to their business, they care little for foreigners, but scoff and laugh at them; and moreover one dare not oppose them, else the streetboys and apprentices collect together in immense crowds and strike to the right and left unmercifully without regard to person; and because they are the strongest, one is obliged to put up with the insult as well as the injury. The women have much more liberty than perhaps in any other place. They also know well how to make use of it, for they go dressed out in exceedingly fine clothes, and give all their attention to their ruffs and stuffs, to such a degree indeed, that, I am informed, many a one does not hesitate to wear velvet in the streets, which is common with them, whilst at home perhaps they have not a piece of dry bread."

or in the kennels where they kept their dogs. In 1563, the people living near Finbury Court put their garbage, including human and animal excrement, into a pile that grew so large that the council of aldermen had to order "the filthy dunghill lying in the highway near unto Finbury Court be removed and carried away."[23]

As a result, rats and other vermin abounded. Laws called for each person to keep his or her property clean, but these were largely ignored, except when the plague struck. Then city authorities made sure garbage was burned. At other times,

people hired the rat catcher, who went from street to street singing:

> Rats or mice, ha' ye any rats or mice,
>   polecats or weasels,
> Or ha' ye any old sows sick of the measles?
> I can kill them, and I can kill moles,
> And I can kill vermin that creepeth up
>   and creepeth down, and peepeth
>   into holes.[24]

Most cities had "scavengers," people hired to keep the streets clean, not only of garbage, but also of the droppings of

Upper stories of houses were built out over the street, shutting out most sunlight, even in daytime. All people were supposed to hang lanterns outside their houses at night, but these lanterns, made of horn and discolored by smoky candles, gave off very little light. Consequently, robbers lurked in the shadows, ready to pounce on the unlucky passerby. Cautious people, if they had to be out after dark, went in groups or hired guards with torches.

Widespread Crime

Criminals were everywhere, especially in the suburbs like Southwark, on the south side of the Thames. These were outside the control of the City of London and its system of constables and watchmen. Enforcement of the law was lax, and prostitution abounded. The crowded streets swarmed with cutpurses and pickpockets. There were even schools for pickpockets, such as the one described by a man of the period:

> There was a school house set up to learn young boys to cut purses. There were hung up two devices, the one was a pocket, the other was a purse. The pocket had in it certain counters, and was hung about the hawks' bells, and over the top did hang a little sacring bell [a small bell used in a church], and he that could take out a counter without any noise was allowed to be a public foyster [thief], and he that could take a piece of silver out of the purse, without the noise of any of the bells, he was adjudged a judicial nipper [pickpocket].[26]

A typical house in London reveals the characteristic English architecture, with the upper stories hanging out over the street.

horses. The city of Oxford hired a person "to carry all sweepings of men's houses and the dirt that cometh of the sweepings of the streets." Every homeowner paid a certain amount every three months "for the carriage [carrying] of the same, and they that have horses to pay for their dung-carriage as the scavenger and they can agree."[25]

Crime was less widespread within London itself but was still more than could be controlled by the watchmen. The streets were so crowded that a pickpocket or cutpurse could easily escape. At night, when the streets were less crowded, criminals would escape notice of the watchmen by taking refuge in jails, bribing the jailers to get a place to sleep until morning.

The River Thames was London's main street. The streets were badly paved (sometimes unpaved) and so crowded that most people used the river if they wanted to get from one part of London to another. The no-

The Plague

Crowded cities in Elizabethan England were breeding grounds for diseases, the deadliest of which was the plague, here described by Thomas Dekker in his Worke for Armourers. *It is found in* The Horizon Book of the Elizabethan World *by Lacey Baldwin Smith.*

"The purple whip of vengeance, the plague, having beaten many thousands of men, women, and children to death, and still marking the people of this city every week by hundreds for the grave, is the only cause that all her inhabitants walk up and down like mourners at some great solemn funeral, the City [London] herself being the chief mourners. The poison of this lingering infection strikes so deep into all men's hearts that their cheeks, like cowardly soldiers, have lost their colors; their eyes, as if they were in debt and durst not look abroad, do scarce peep out of their heads; and their tongues, like physicians ill-paid, give but cold comfort. By the power of their pestilent charms all merry meetings are cut off, all frolic assemblies dissolved, and in their circles are raised up the black, sullen, and dogged spirits of sadness, of melancholy, and so, consequently, of mischief. Mirth is departed and lies dead and buried in men's bosoms; laughter dares not look a man in the face; jests are, like music to the deaf, not regarded; pleasure itself finds now no pleasure by in sighing and bewailing the miseries of the time. For, alack! what string is there now to be played upon whose touch can make us merry? Playhouses stand like taverns that have cast out their masters, the doors locked up, the flags, like their bushes, taken down—or rather like houses lately infected, from whence the affrighted dwellers are fled, in hope to live better in the country."

The River Thames functioned as a main street in sixteenth-century London. Many houses were built alongside the river for easy access. The other main avenue was London Bridge, which can be seen in the background.

ble houses along the Strand, the main road between London and Westminster, backed up to the river, and the residents kept their own boats at private docks. Ordinary citizens paid wherrymen (boatmen) to row them where they wanted to go. It was much quicker and cleaner than going by land.

The river, however, was not much cleaner than the streets. Despite numerous attempts to stop the practice, people dumped garbage and raw sewage into the Thames. Butchers used it to dispose of the

bodies and unusable parts of cattle, sheep, and pigs. As a result, the Thames stank to the point where a visitor from Italy wrote that its "odour remains even in clean linen" after being washed.[27]

London Bridge was the only other way to cross the river. This marvelous structure was thought to be one of the wonders of the time. It was covered from bank to bank and lined with fashionable shops and houses. There was even a church halfway across. Above the gatehouse at the south end of London Bridge, the rotting heads of persons executed as traitors were stuck on poles. A visitor in 1594 counted thirty-four such grim reminders of the queen's justice.

The Excitement of London

Yet, for all its squalor, Elizabethan London could be an exciting place. The great theaters, including Shakespeare's Globe, were built in the suburbs on the south bank of the Thames. Even St. Paul's Cathedral, one of the largest churches in Europe, was lively. Besides being a house of worship, it was used as a place for business, gossip, plotting, and for lovers to meet. A visitor described the scene in Paul's Walk, the great middle aisle of the church:

> What swearing is there, what facing and out-facing? What shuffling, what shouldering, what jostling, what jeering, what biting of thumbs to beget quarrels . . . what casting open of cloaks to publish new clothes, what muffling in cloaks to hide broken elbows . . . foot by foot and elbow by elbow shall you see walking the knight, the gull, the gallant, the upstart, the gentleman, the clown, the captain, the apple-squire, the lawyer, the usurer, the citizen, the bankrupt, the scholar, the beggar, the doctor, the idiot, the ruffian, the cheater, the Puritan, the cut-throat.[28]

Everything was for sale in London. John Lyly described it in 1579 as "a place both for the beauty of building, infinite riches, variety of all things, that excelleth all the cities in the world, insomuch that it may be called the storehouse and mart of all Europe."[29] London's version of the shopping mall was the Royal Exchange, built in 1567 as a place for merchants to show their wares. As a poem of the time said:

Merchants flocked to London's Royal Exchange, where those who showed their wares often ended the day with satisfying profits.

Such purses, gloves and points
Of cost and fashion rare,
Such cutworks, partlets, suits of lawn,
Bongraces and such ware;
Such gorgets, sleeves and ruffs,
Linings for gowns and cauls,
Coifs, cirppins, cornets, billaments,
Musk boxes and sweet balls;
Pincases, pick-tooths, beard-brushes,
Combs, needles, glasses, bells,
and many such like toys as these,
That Gain to Fancy sells.[30]

A Hungry Giant

London was so much the center of business that other English cities complained. Merchants in Norwich, Bristol, Newcastle, Southampton, and the rest claimed London was swallowing the entire country's trade. While it was true that merchants had to bring their goods to London to sell them to foreign buyers, they did, in fact, turn a tidy profit there that they took back home. Almost all the English cities prospered far more under Elizabeth than under her predecessors because of the growth of trade and manufacturing throughout the entire kingdom.

The cities were growing in independence. Elizabeth granted many more royal charters to cities and towns than did her predecessors. A charter set forth the extent to which a city could govern itself and be free from the authority of neighboring nobles. It also said what taxes, tolls, and other payments the cities could collect. The cities usually paid for these documents, providing the queen with revenue.

Part of the cities' growing power was their increased representation in Parliament. Elizabeth created thirty-two new boroughs, each of which had the right to send two members to Parliament. Because Parliament was not, under the Tudors, the all-powerful legislative body it would later become, the cities often let nearby landowners represent them—provided they could pay their own way. Only the largest cities were willing to pay the expenses for two members of Parliament, and few of the leading merchants were willing to leave their businesses and go to London to serve during a session that might last anywhere from a few weeks to half a year.

The cities, which for centuries had feuded mainly with local nobles, now argued instead with one another. Their new prosperity led to arguments over who had the right to fish in what waters, who had the right to sell what on market day, who had the right to call out troops. The cities were jealous of the privileges they thought both tradition and their charters allowed them. Newcomers who wanted to set up businesses were not welcome. "Wherare other cities doe alure unto them goode workmen," wrote one haughty citizen, "our men will expell theim oute."[31]

While the cities dominated commerce, they did not, except for London, dominate the countryside around them. The most important accomplishment of the cities in the Elizabethan Era was the measure of independence that was gained by the people. As historian A. L. Rowse wrote, "The towns ran themselves, but they did not run the country."[32]

Chapter

3 Life in the Countryside

Despite the growth of the cities, England was still mostly rural in the Elizabethan Age. Eight of every ten people lived in the countryside. Trade and commerce were growing, but agriculture remained the dominant industry. The second half of the sixteenth century saw fundamental changes in farming—changes that would be reflected in the life of the country.

For centuries, farming in England had been done "in common." People would agree with a local nobleman to work so many days on his land in exchange for the right to farm the "common," land still owned by the nobleman but on which tenants raised food and livestock for their own use. The common, also called "champion" land, was open and unfenced. Each family had its own scattered half-acre strips of cropland. This was "subsistence" farming—everything raised went to feed the family, with perhaps a little left over to take to market.

The nature of farming began to change in the 1400s and was sped up during Elizabeth's reign by the growth of cities. More and more, landowners were not farmers in the traditional sense, raising food to feed their families. They were out to make money by raising crops to sell to the growing number of town dwellers. This led to an entirely new type of landlord. Unlike the noblemen, who had a certain responsibility for the welfare of their workers, the new landlord might live in another part of the country. He would very likely be a merchant rather than a nobleman, first, because there were far fewer noblemen than before (because of the Wars of the Roses), and second, because the merchants would

Wheat is harvested during the sixteenth century. Although cities were becoming more important, most people lived in the countryside during the Elizabethan Era.

be more likely to have the cash to buy land. The merchant might have bought former monastery land as an investment. He would make money any way he could.

A Wasteful Tradition

Farming in common was very inefficient. Plowing, instead of being done in long rows on large fields, was done in tiny, crisscrossed strips. The "balks," the areas between the strips, were wasted. Because an individual family's strips were in different places around the common (so that nobody would get all of the most fertile ground), time was wasted going from one strip to another. Each family usually owned a few head of cat-

tle and, because the cattle all grazed together, owners could not try to improve their animals through selective breeding. There was more danger of the spread of disease among animals because the sick were not isolated from the rest of the herd.

Eventually, people realized it would be much more efficient for each farmer to consolidate his fields and grazing land and to surround them with fences, usually of thick hedges. This method was known as farming "in several" and the use of fences as "enclosure." There is no doubt that it was more efficient. Thomas Tusser, whose *Hundred Points of Good Husbandry* was an Elizabethan best-seller, wrote:

More profit is quieter found
Where pastures in several be

Evils of Enclosure

This poem by the Rev. Thomas Bastard, written in 1598, deplores the ruin of villages through the enclosure of land. It is found in Elizabethan People: State and Society.

I know where is a thief and long hath been,
Which spoileth every place where he resorts:
He steals away both subjects from the Queen,
And men from his own country of all sorts.
Houses by three, and seven, and ten he raseth
   [tears down],
To make the common glebe [fields] his private land:
Our country cities cruel he defaceth,
The grass grows green where little Troy did stand,
The forlorn father hanging down his head,
His outcast company drawn up and down,
The pining labourer doth beg his bread,
The plowswain seeks his dinner from the town.
O Prince, the wrong is thine, for understand,
Many such robberies will undo thy land.

Of one silly acre of ground
Than champion maketh of three.[33]

Enclosure was efficient, but it resulted in a great deal of social upheaval. In the first half of the century, the price of English wool had been very high. To take advantage of this, many of the new, profit-minded landowners enclosed their fields and turned cropland into pasture for sheep. To do this, they first had to get rid of the families who had been farming the land. "Freeholders"—those tenants of the landlord who had long leases or fixed rents—were fairly safe. Most tenants, however, paid rents that could be raised at any time. Landlords raised these rents to the point where the tenants could not pay. They then were expelled from the land on which their ancestors might have lived for generations. Thousands of people were thrown out of work. Entire villages disappeared.

Enclosure continued under Elizabeth, but with a different emphasis. The price of wool fell and the price of food—because of a greater demand resulting from increased population—increased. Now, raising crops became more profitable than raising sheep, and many landowners turned their pastures back into cropland. Rather than a return to the common land system, however, farming was done in larger, enclosed fields requiring fewer workers.

The Problem of the Unemployed

The small tenant farmers who lost their land could, if they were lucky, stay on as hired laborers. Their wives might find positions as cooks or servants in the land-

A shepherd watches over his grazing sheep. English wool and textiles were known throughout Europe for their exquisite quality.

lord's house. The unlucky ones joined the swelling number of those who wandered from place to place, looking for any kind of work. Up to now, virtually every person had had a specific place in the economic order, either on the land or in a craft. The large-scale unemployment brought about by enclosure was something new in England.

The government was afraid that this unemployment would lead to a rebellion.

Land Grabbers

"There is not life more pleasant than a yeoman's life, but nowadays yeomanry is decayed, hospitality gone to wrack and husbandry almost quite fallen. The reason is because landlords, not contented with such revenues as their predecessors received, nor yet satisfied that they live like swinish epicures quietly at their ease, doing no good to the commonwealth, do leave no ground for tillage, but do enclose for pasture many thousand acres of ground within one hedge, the husbandmen are thrust out of their own, or else by deceit constrained to sell all they have."

Claiming the "strength and flourishing estate of this kingdom" depended on farming—"being a principal mean that people are set on work"—the government passed laws to limit enclosures and keep as many people as possible on the land.[34] The trouble was that the local officials in charge of enforcing the laws were often the same men who profited from enclosure. No wonder the laws had little effect and were seldom enforced.

Near the close of Elizabeth's reign, the land was able to produce far more crops than at first. For one thing, farming in several was more efficient. For another, the change from subsistence to cash farming enabled each area of the country to specialize. Farmers no longer had to grow everything they needed for their own use. They could grow only the crops best suited to their soil and climate. Southern England, for instance, was famous for its fruit—apples, pears, and cherries.

Significantly, root crops—beets, turnips, and carrots—were not grown, except in gardens for human use. One of the problems of Elizabethan agriculture was feeding livestock in the winter. Only so many could be fed; the rest were slaughtered for food. Because meat could not be preserved very well, there was plenty to eat through Christmas and not much afterward. Tusser wrote:

> At Hallowtide slaughter time entereth in
>   and then doth the husbandman's feastings begin;
> From thence until Shrovetide kill now
>   and then some,
>   their offal for household the better
>   will come. . . .
> Beef, mutton and pork, shred pies of
>   the best,
>   pig, veal, goose and capon, and
>   turkey well drest;
> Cheese, apples and nuts, jolly carols to
>   hear,

as then in the country is counted good cheer.[35]

No one had yet thought of growing large quantities of root crops to feed the animals through the winter. This was not done for another hundred years.

Methods of Farming

Methods of farming were still very primitive. Plows were made of wood, although a few had iron blades. They were pulled mostly by oxen instead of horses. Most farmers fashioned their tools themselves out of whatever was available. A thorn bush might be used as a harrow to rake the ground.

People knew that planting one crop year after year made the soil infertile, and they practiced crop rotation—changing the crop in a field each year and leaving it "fallow," unplanted, every third or fourth year. Fertilizer was used, but instead of manure, it usually consisted of ash, decayed vegetable matter, or types of earth—such as peat and loam—known to be rich in minerals. No effort was made to use the huge amounts of animal waste from London and the cities until the following century.

Elizabethan farmers were eager to learn how to get more from their land. Books on agriculture were popular. Tusser wrote the *Hundred Points of Good Husbandry* in 1557. Thirteen editions of the book were printed. It was highly popular because Tusser, who had been a court musician before he became a farmer, wrote the entire book in verse. Here, for instance, is how to keep the house free of fleas:

A farmer plows his field with the help of oxen. Farmers were continually trying to improve their methods, often turning to books that offered advice.

While wormwood hath seed, get a
    bundle or twain,
To save against March, to make flea
    refrain.
Where chamber is swept and that
    wormwood is strown,
No flea for his life dare abide to be
    known.[36]

A Dreary Existence

The lives of the poor farmers and their families, in addition to being hard, were uncertain. Many of them lived from month to month, never sure if they would be able to produce enough food to feed themselves, never certain if they would be able to stay on their land. William Harrison, writing at the time, said the poor tenant farmer counted himself lucky if he could keep a roof over his head and have enough land to plant "cabbages, radishes, parsnips, carrots, melons, pumpkins . . . by which he and his poor household liveth as their principal food, sith [since] they can do no better."[37]

The lives of the poor were also very monotonous and dull. Their work left them little time for recreation. Their only entertainment was at the occasional village fair or church festival. They seldom left their village, perhaps traveling once or twice a year to the nearest market town. They obtained their news of the outside world from travelers or peddlers.

The lives of the more well-to-do landowners were more comfortable, but hardly easy. Unless he were extremely wealthy and had a bailiff or steward, the landowner had to personally oversee everything from planting to harvesting. His wife supervised the household, which—counting laborers and servants—could number as many as a hundred people. Everyone rose at dawn (except on Sunday) and went to bed early. As Tusser wrote:

A Law for Crops

Three wet summers in a row created bad harvests and a food shortage toward the close of Elizabeth's reign. This Act of Parliament in 1598 called for more land to be used for crops and less for raising sheep. It is found in Elizabethan People: State and Society.

"Be it enacted . . . that whereas any lands or grounds at any time since the seventeenth of November in the first year of her Majesty's reign have been converted to sheep pastures or to the fattening or grazing of cattle, the same lands having been tillable lands, fields or grounds such as have been used in tillage or for tillage by the space of twelve years together at the least next before such conversion, according to the nature of the soil and course of husbandry used in that part of the country, all such lands and grounds as aforesaid shall, before the first day of May which shall be in the year of Our Lord God one thousand five hundred and ninety nine, be restored to tillage, or laid for tillage in such sort as the whole ground, according to the nature of that soil and course of husbandry used in that part of the country, be within three years at the lease turned to tillage by the occupiers and possessors thereof, and so shall be continued for ever."

In winter at nine and in summer at ten
To bed after supper both maidens
and men.[38]

The year was a never-ending cycle of work. The typical farmer would spend December putting his tools in good working order. Preparation of his fields began in January. Crops were planted in March and April, the same month as his lambs were born. The sheep were sheared in June, the hay harvested in July, the corn har- vested in August, the fruit gathered in September, and October and November spent storing up food for the winter.

The ordinary country farmer, unlike his nobleman neighbor, probably would not have had much education. His wife probably had less. When a teacher was available, he was most likely the local par- son or the parish clerk. The typical farmer, described by Nicholas Breton, learned just enough to get by:

The average country farm family lived in a simple cottage. Both the man and woman of the house worked long hours and had little time for recreation or travel.

Wealthy families lived in richly decorated manor houses on large estates. Servants performed most household duties, stewards attended to the land, and private tutors saw to the educational needs of the nobleman's children.

This is all we go to school for—to read Common Prayers at Church, and set down common prices at markets; write a letter, and make a bond; set down the day of our births, our marriage day, and make our wills when we are sick, for the disposing of our goods when we are dead. . . . We can learn to plough and harrow, sow and reap, plant and prune, thrash and fan, winnow and grind, brew and bake, and all without book; and these are our chief business in the country.[39]

The nobleman, however, would hire private tutors for his children. He lived in a great castle or manor house. His walls might be hung with rich tapestries, while his less wealthy neighbor would probably have bacon and hams hanging from his rafters. The nobleman would seldom attend to his land himself, but would leave the work to a steward while he went to court in London.

The noblemen looked down on the hard-working farmers who slowly were growing more wealthy. As the farmers prospered, they were able to enlarge their houses, wear finer clothes, and hire more workers. In his description of the country, John Norden pokes fun at common farmers who "wade in the weeds [clothes] of gentlemen."[40] And a poem of the time denounces "upstart gentlemen," saying:

> For those that of late did sup
> Out of an ashen [wooden] cup
> Are wonderfully sprung up;
> That nought was worth of late.[41]

4 Social Classes and Government

The English of the Elizabethan Age had a strong sense of order and stability. The economic forces of the time, however, blurred the lines between social classes, and families could—and frequently did—move from one level to another.

The nobility, the highest level, was smaller under the Tudors than in previous centuries. Many noble families had been killed off during the Wars of the Roses. Elizabeth saw the nobility as a potential threat to her power and preferred to keep the number of nobles small. Noble titles could be acquired in two ways: by inheritance and by a grant from the monarch. Elizabeth created very few noblemen during her reign. The two chief examples were William Cecil, made Lord Burghley, and Robert Dudley, created Earl of Leicester.

The granting of noble titles for service to the crown was fairly new in England and almost unknown in the rest of Europe, where ancestry defined nobility. The nobles created for service to the Tudors were looked down on by the older nobility as "new men." Sir Francis Bacon wrote, "For new nobility is but the act of power; but ancient nobility is the act of time."[42]

Nobility, whether new or old, carried with it a certain permanence. Titles were hereditary, passing from father to oldest son. Members of other classes might lose their status by squandering their fortunes, but it took a crime such as treason for a nobleman to lose his title.

Elizabeth endowed William Cecil with the title Lord Burghley. Afraid of the power of the nobles, Elizabeth created very few during her time.

The nobility lived luxuriously. They had no choice. As historian A. H. Dodd wrote, "While the simple gentleman [wealthy but not noble] might live like a lord, the lord could not live like a simple gentleman without losing face."[43] Nobles were expected to be lavish in their dress, their houses, and their habits. They were expected to serve in an office, such as being an ambassador to a foreign country, at their own expense.

The days when the nobility ran the country were gone forever. From Tudor times on, they had to share power with the gentry and the great merchants. Still, they had enormous influence. Most of Elizabeth's council came from the nobility, and the chief officers in the counties—such as the Lord-Lieutenants and sheriffs—usually came from noble families.

The Gentry

The next level of society, and the most important during the Elizabethan Era, was the gentry. Wealth was the key to becoming part of the gentry. These were people not of noble birth who, by acquiring large amounts of property, became wealthy landowners. Some families bought property bit by bit over generations. A man might marry the daughter of a lesser knight or noble and gain land through his wife's inheritance. Some of the great merchants made their fortunes in the city, then bought a country estate.

The upper gentry lived like nobles, building huge houses, and employing hundreds of servants. They could not buy their way into the nobility, but their sons or grandsons often became peers (nobles). A good example of the social mobil-

Although class differences were prominent during Elizabeth's time, ordinary citizens could rise in class rank. Sir Walter Raleigh was one of those who rose from peasant stock to gentry.

ity of the century is Burghley. His grandfather was a man-at-arms under Henry VII, his father was knighted, he was made a baron, and his son was made an earl; each generation earned a title higher than the one before.

The gentry were the backbone of Elizabethan England. They combined the wealth of the nobility with the energy of the sturdy peasants from whom they had sprung. Historian A. L. Rowse wrote:

The rise of the gentry was the dominant feature of Elizabethan society. It was they essentially who changed things, who launched out along new paths whether at home or overseas, who achieved what was achieved, who gave what all societies need—leadership. One may fairly say that most of the leading spirits of the age, those who gave it its character and did its work, were of this class.[44]

Examples were everywhere. Two of the queen's chief ministers, Burghley and Walsingham, were products of the gentry. Francis Bacon, the great essayist and philosopher, came from this class. So did John Hawkins and Francis Drake, the famous explorers. So did Walter Raleigh, the man who led the way to the English colonization of America.

The gentry were the solid citizens of Elizabethan England. They went to Parliament and served as Justices of the Peace. Some were vain about their status. They applied to

Social Classes

In his Description of England, *written during Elizabeth's reign, William Harrison gave this description of society. It appears in* Elizabethan People: State and Society.

"We in England divide our people commonly into four sorts, as gentlemen, citizens or burgesses, yeomen, and artificers or labourers. Of gentlemen the first and chief (next the King) be the prince, dukes, marquises, earls, viscounts, and barons, and these are called gentlemen of the greater sort, or (as our common usage of speech is) lords and noblemen; and next unto them be knights, esquires, and, last of all, they that are simply called gentlemen. . . . Citizens and burgesses have next place to gentlemen, who be those that are free within the cities, and are of some likely substance to bear office in the same. . . . Yeomen are those which by our law are called *legales homines,* freemen born English, and may dispend of their own free land in yearly revenue to the sum of 40s. sterling, or £6 as money goeth in our times. . . . The fourth and last sort of people in England are day labourers, poor husbandmen, and some retailers (which have no free land), copyholders, and all artificers, as tailors, shoemakers, carpenters, brickmakers, masons, etc. As for slaves and bondmen, we have none, nay such is the privilege of our country by the especial grace of God and bounty of our princes that if any come hither from other realms, so soon as they set foot on land they become so free of condition as their masters."

the College of Heralds for family coats of arms, sometimes on the strength of a fabricated family tree. Others were not at all ashamed of their own roots. Robert Furse, an Elizabethan gentleman, wrote of his ancestors that

> although some of them were but simple and unlearned and men of small possessions . . . for I am sure that the greatest ox was first a little calf and the mightiest oak a small branch or little twig and the great river . . . a little spring of water; but by keeping of his own course and within his own bounds it groweth by little and little so that at last it is become an exceeding great river.[45]

The Yeomen

The men from whom the gentry came were the yeomen, the next and most unique of Elizabethan England's social classes. The yeomen were the small farmers "living in the temperate zone betwixt greatness and want."[46] They had existed for centuries and were, like the gentry, peculiar to England. They had no counterparts in Europe, which had great nobles, poor peasants, and little in between.

The yeomen were prosperous, and their wealth could exceed that of some of the gentry. The difference was how they spent their wealth. The gentry lived like lords, building great houses. The yeoman was content to live more simply, using his wealth to improve his land and to expand it. The yeoman, wrote Elizabethan official William Lambarde, "although otherwise for wealth comparable with the gentle sort that will not yet for all that change their

The yeomen held a unique place in Elizabethan society. Many amassed great wealth but chose to live more simply than the free-spending gentry.

condition, nor desire to be apparelled with the titles of gentry."[47]

The gentry and the yeomen were considered freeholders, although they might lease their property from a noble rather than owning it outright. The leases, however, were for long periods (up to ninety-nine years) at a fixed rate. Below them on the social scale were the small leaseholders. They were known both as "customary" tenants, because their ancestors had held the same land by tradition from a lord, or "copyholders," because they could demonstrate their claim to the land by showing a copy of some document showing the original terms of the lease.

The copyholder's lands might occasionally compare in size and wealth with those

English "Gentlemen"

Thomas Smith, in his De Republica Anglorum [Of the English Republic] *written in the 1560s, had this low opinion of some in England who had lately become gentlemen. It is found in* Elizabethan People: State and Society.

"As for gentlemen, they be made good cheap in England. For whosoever studieth the laws of the realm, who studieth in the universities, who professeth liberal sciences, and to be short, who can live idly and without manual labour and will bear the port [bearing], charge [cost] and countenance of a gentleman, he shall be called master, for that is the title which men give to esquires and other gentlemen, and shall be taken for a gentleman. . . . And if need be if a king of heralds shall also give him for money [a coat of] arms newly made and invented, the title whereof shall pretend to have been found by the said herald in perusing and viewing of old registers, where his ancestors in times past had been recorded to bear the same. Or if he will do it more truly and of better faith, he will write that for the merits of that man, and certain qualities which he doth see in him, and for sundry noble acts which he hath performed, he by the authority which he hath as king of heralds and arms, giveth to him and his heirs these and these arms, which being done I think he may be called a squire, for he beareth ever after those arms."

of the yeoman, but he was much less secure. His lease might be for life, in which case he could not be sure his son would inherit the land. His lease might be hereditary, but the amount due to the landowner might change. In either case, copyholders frequently were forced off their land to make way for the large, enclosed operations.

Beneath the copyholders were the hired laborers. Some of these lived in one place, working for wages on the lord's land and farming the four acres that, by law, went with their cottages. Other laborers went from county to county as migrant workers, wherever there might be sheep to shear or crops to harvest.

The Poor

At the bottom were the poor. There was far more poverty under Elizabeth than in previous reigns, mostly because of enclosure, but there were also the sick, the disabled, the old and feeble, and soldiers unable to work because of wounds. In earlier times, the church—notably the monasteries—

had cared for the poor. Under Elizabeth, the government undertook the job—a big job because enclosure had created so much unemployment.

The result was the famous Elizabethan Poor Laws, one of the world's first government-sponsored welfare programs. The program was financed, at first, by contributions from the wealthy. When this proved inadequate, a poor tax was levied on everyone. The Poor Laws had three goals: First, those unable to care for themselves were placed in hospitals or orphanages. Children, when they were old enough, were put out as apprentices to craftsmen. Second, the able-bodied who could not find jobs on their own were put to work, usually in workhouses established in the towns. These were places where the unemployed

Elizabeth was the first English monarch to use the powers of government to care for the poor. Her Poor Laws were innovative and effective.

were put to work making goods for sale—such small items as candles, soap, or rope—in exchange for a place to sleep and enough food to keep alive.

The third goal was to discourage the permanently unemployed—"rogues, vagabonds, and sturdy beggars" responsible for "horrible murders, thefts, and other great outrages."[48] The Elizabethans made a clear distinction between those who, for one reason or another, were unable to work and those able-bodied people who refused employment, whether in a regular job or in a workhouse. The Elizabethan sense of order revolted at the thought of people wandering about with no respectable occupation. To refuse to work for wages was an offense punishable by law. When vagrants were caught, they were whipped and returned to the parishes (church areas) of their birth. William Lambarde wrote of such a case:

> John at Stile, a sturdy vagrant beggar, of low personage, red-haired and having the nail of his right thumb cloven, was the sixth day of April in the forty and one year of the reign of our sovereign lady Queen Elizabeth openly whipped at Dale in the said county for a wandering rogue according to the law, and is assigned to pass forthwith from parish to parish by the officers thereof the next straight way to Sale in the county of Middlesex, where (as he confesseth) he was born . . . and he is limited to be at Sale aforesaid within ten days now next ensuing at his peril.[49]

If the vagrant refused work or escaped from a workhouse and was caught, he was "burned through the gristle of the right ear with a hot iron of the compass of an inch about."[50] If, for a third time, a vagrant

The Poor

A growing problem in the Elizabethan Era was the increasing number of poor people. Scholar William Lambarde wrote about it in his 1594 book Eirenarcha. *This excerpt is found in* Elizabethan People: State and Society.

"The dearth of all things maketh likewise many poor, and that cometh either by the excessive enhancement of the rents of land, which hath now invaded the lands both of the church and Crown itself, or by that foul and cancerous sore of daily usury, which is already run and spread over all the body of the commonwealth, or by our immoderate use, or rather abuse, of foreign commodities, the which we (breaking all symmetry and good proportion) do make as vile and common unto us as our own domestical. But whether these only, or chiefly, or they with some other be the true causes of dearth, that is a disputation for another time, place, and assembly. These I note that every man may have a conscience in them, lest through his fault dearth grow and consequently the number of poor be increased by it. Lastly, the poor are exceedingly much multiplied because for the most part all the whole children and brood of the poor be poor also, seeing that they are not taken from their wandering parents and brought up to honest labour for their living but, following their idle steps . . . as they be born and brought up, so do they live and die, most shameless and shameful rogues and beggars."

was found to be unemployed, the punishment was death.

Government by All Classes

England's government was unusual among European monarchies in that its officials came from virtually every level of society. Even copyholders "be commonly made church-wardens, ale-conners, and many times constables, which office toucheth more the commonwealth."[51] The English had a strong inclination toward self-government instead of dictatorship. The government of the Elizabethan Age developed into an efficient balance among the queen, the nobility, the merchants, and the gentry.

Elizabeth was a strong ruler, but she knew her people well enough not to be an absolute monarch—one whose every word was law. Her successors, the Stuarts, held the theory that kings had a "divine right" to rule and brought on a revolution. Eliza-

Elizabethan society distinguished between the able-bodied and disabled poor. If beggars such as these were found to be able-bodied, they were exiled to the village in which they were born.

beth, as A. L. Rowse wrote, "had less learning and more sense."[52]

Elizabeth decided all great questions of policy, but her council conducted most of the actual work of government. She was clever enough to keep members of the council at odds with one another so they would not dominate her. Burghley was her chief adviser, but she often instead took the advice of Burghley's rival, Leicester. Thus, she "ruled much by faction and parties, which herself both made, upheld and weakened, as her own great judgment advised."[53]

Elizabeth's council worked hard, eventually meeting every day of the week, sometimes twice a day. Their workload was tremendous because they dealt both with matters of national urgency and with the

smallest cases. For example, in the same week the council was preparing for a threatened invasion by Spain in 1588—sending orders to the fleet, positioning troops, seeing to the defense of the kingdom—it dealt with the punishment of one Gill of Brighton, found guilty of criticizing an admiral, and with the finding of some Catholic priests' robes near Reading.

The council could not pass laws; that was Parliament's job. Parliament did not meet on a regular basis but was called by the queen when the need arose. Elizabeth did not enjoy calling Parliament. It tended to give her unwanted advice regarding who to marry or to press her to name her successor. She needed money, however, to fight wars in the Netherlands with Spain, and the regular sources of royal income—from land owned by the crown, from fees and fines, from certain import and export duties—were not enough. Special taxes were needed, and taxes—by long tradition—were levied by Parliament.

Parliament's Self-Awareness

As a result, Parliament met often during Elizabeth's reign and began to get a sense of its own importance. Members began to question why they must deal only with matters as ordered by the queen, with no right to bring up other issues. One member, Peter Wentworth, asked Parliament to decide

whether the Prince and State can be maintained without this court of Parliament? Whether there be any council that can make or abrogate [abolish] laws, but only this court of Parliament? Whether free speech and free doings

On Keeping the Peace

The essayist Sir Francis Bacon, in his Essays or Counsels, Civil and Moral, *gave this opinion on how a country's internal unrest can be prevented. It is found in* The Horizon Book of the Elizabethan World *by Lacey Baldwin Smith.*

"The causes of motives of seditions [treasons] are innovation in religion, taxes, alteration of laws and customs, breaking of privileges, general oppression, advancement of unworthy persons, strangers, dearths, disbanded soldiers, factions grown desperate, and whatsoever in offending people joineth and knitteth them in a common cause. . . . The first remedy or prevention is to remove by all means possible that material cause of sedition whereof we spake, which is want and poverty in the estate. To which purpose serveth the opening and well-balancing of trade, the cherishing of manufactures, the banishing of idleness, the repressing of waste and excess by sumptuary laws [which controlled how richly people were allowed to live], the improvement and husbanding of the soil, the regulating of prices of things vendible, the moderating of taxes and tributes and the like. Generally, it is to be foreseen that the population of a kingdome (especially if it be not mown down by wars) to not exceed the stock of the kingdom which should maintain them. Neither is the population to be reckoned with only by number, for a smaller number that spend more and earn less do wear out an estate sooner than a greater number that live lower and gather more. Therefore the multiplying of nobility and other degrees of quality in an over proportion to the common people doth speedily bring a state to necessity, and so doth likewise an overgrown clergy, for they bring nothing to the stock; and in like manner, when more are bred scholars than preferments can take care of. . . . Above all things, good policy is to be used that the treasure and monies in a state be not gathered into few hands, for otherwise a state may have a great stock and yet starve. And money is like much, not good except it be spread."

A session of Parliament operates under Elizabeth's watchful eye. Even though Parliament had the power to pass laws, its authority was subject to approval by the queen.

Elizabeth's council administered the law through a network of local officials. The Lord-Lieutenants, usually members of the nobility, made up the highest level. As many as seventeen Lord-Lieutenants carried out the work of the council in England's twenty-nine counties. Much of the work of the Lord-Lieutenants was military. They were responsible for raising, arming, and training troops. The Lord-Lieutenants also had financial responsibilities, such as collecting involuntary "loans" ordered by the council when money was needed in an emergency.

The officials most concerned with everyday life were the Justices of the Peace. These men, whose workload was heavy and who were not paid any salary, served for the honor of the position and for the good of the country. Their duties ranged from enforcing the Poor Laws to stopping illegal games (such as football). As Rowse wrote, "There were very few corners in local life into which J.P.s might not pry."[55]

More serious crimes, however, were tried by the justices of the High Courts of Justice. These royal courts heard cases, not only at Westminster, but also throughout the country in sessions known as "assizes." There were few prisons, so long jail sentences were rare. The local jail was a place to hold a prisoner until he or she could be brought to trial.

. . . be not granted to every one of the Parliament house by law?[54]

In other words, Wentworth was asking whether Parliament should be free to pass whatever laws it wished and free to act independently of the monarch and the council. These questions were to be answered by the revolution in the next century.

Punishment

Most offenders were quickly punished. For small crimes, such as not attending church, fines were collected. A woman found guilty of disturbing the peace might be strapped into a chair at the end of a

The Power of Parliament

In his De Republica Anglorum, *Thomas Smith set forth his description of the authority of Parliament. By "Parliament," Smith meant Parliament with the sanction of the king or queen. The passage is found in* Elizabethan People: State and Society.

"The most high and absolute power of the realm of England consisteth in the parliament. For in war where the king himself in person, the nobility, the rest of the gentility and the yeomanry are, is the force and power of England, so in peace and consultation where the prince is to give life and the last and highest commandment, the barony for the nobility and higher, the knights, squires, gentlemen and commons for the lower part of the commonwealth, the bishops for the clergy, be present to advertise consult and shew what is good and necessary for the commonwealth and to consult together, and upon mature deliberation every bill or law being thrice read and disputed in either house, the other two parts first each apart, and after the prince [king or queen] himself in presence of both the parties doth consent unto and alloweth. That is the prince's and whole realm's deed, whereupon justly no man can complain, but must accommodate himself to find it good and obey it. That which is done by this consent is called firm, stable, and *sanctum* [hallowed] and is taken for law. The parliament abrogateth [revokes] old laws, maketh new, giveth orders for things past, and for things hereafter to be followed. . . . And, to be short, all that ever the people of Rome might do . . . the same may be done by the parliament of England, which representeth and hath the power of the whole realm both the head and the body."

Parliament in session. During Elizabeth's reign, the government body was already chafing under the monarch's control.

long pole and dunked into the village pond. A man arrested for drunkenness might have to spend a day in the stocks—standing in humiliation with his hands and head securely held in wooden blocks. Crimes slightly more serious, such as vagrancy or fighting, might be punished by a public whipping. Capital punishment was common. Not only murder, but also theft—such as the stealing of a horse or the burglary of a house—was punishable by death. In 1598, seventy-four persons were hanged in the county of Devon alone.

There were many other local positions. The Sheriff was a person of importance just under the Lord-Lieutenant and was chiefly concerned with collecting fees and debts, such as fines levied against Catholics, rents from royal lands, and taxes that had not been paid. The Coroner was responsible for investigating sudden and mysterious deaths. Churchwardens were in charge of church property—such as prayer books, cups and plates used in services, robes worn by the clergy—and constables aided the Justices of the Peace.

Law and government, as practiced under Elizabeth, was perhaps the country's most important achievement. The spirit of cooperation between government and people was found nowhere else in Europe. People at almost every level of society par-

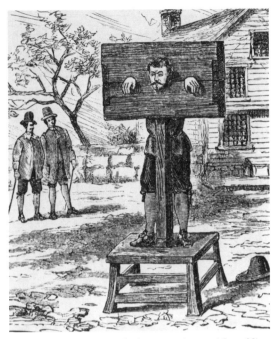

Elizabethan law punished many crimes with public humiliation. The stocks were a common punishment for minor crimes such as public drunkenness.

ticipated in the process. The concept of government with the consent of the governed would eventually extend to the United States. Rowse wrote, "If English-speaking people anywhere want to know the source of the self-government which is their peculiar contribution to the world in the sphere of politics, it is to be found as far back as the Tudor tradition."[56]

5 Religion and the Church

When Elizabeth became queen, the country anxiously waited to see what form religion would take. Under her father and brother, England had left the Catholic church, only to return under Queen Mary I's reign. The Church of England, as it emerged under Elizabeth, was an expression of her views and those of most of her people—moderate, conservative, and surprisingly tolerant. What came to be known as the Elizabethan Religious Settlement was to have a profound effect on the country.

Religion was the center of everyday life just as much in Elizabethan England as it had been for centuries. It raised passions like nothing else. People might be ardent Catholics, or resolute Puritans, or even firm atheists (denying the existence of God), but almost no one was indifferent.

The English had been pulled this way and that over religion for twenty-five years. Not only were the people confused, they were also afraid. Hundreds of people, Catholic and Protestant, mighty and humble,

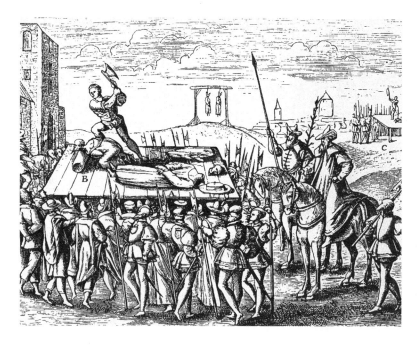

A person of the Catholic faith is beheaded during the reign of Henry VIII. Many of England's rulers showed little tolerance for religious beliefs different from their own.

had been executed for their beliefs. Above all, the people wanted and needed peace. The Duke of Norfolk advised Elizabeth, "Let your highness assure yourself that England can bear no more changes in religion. It hath been bowed so oft that if it should be bent again it would break."[57]

Much depended on Elizabeth's personal beliefs. In her brother's reign, she had been a demure, pious Protestant. In her sister's, she attended Catholic mass dutifully, if unenthusiastically. Elizabeth's personal religion was a simple, rational belief that did not go to either Catholic or Protestant extremes. This middle-of-the-road approach was totally in keeping with the uncertainty through which Elizabeth had lived under both Edward and Mary. Once, she wrote:

Christ was the word that spake it,
He took the bread and brake it;
And what his words did make it
That I believe and take it.[58]

A Limit to Toleration

Elizabeth was by no means tolerant of all Christians. She found both extreme Catholics and extreme Protestants distasteful. She took action against them, however, only when their beliefs posed a political threat, such as when some Catholics wanted to replace her with Mary Queen of Scots or when the Anabaptists, an extreme Protestant sect, preached complete separation of church and state.

Elizabeth probably could not have kept England Catholic even if she had wanted to. The persecutions under Queen Mary had produced a fierce hatred of

Elizabeth in prayer. Although she could not tolerate religious extremists of any type, Elizabeth maintained a firm belief in treating personal religion as a private, not a state matter.

Spain because the people believed she was guided by her Spanish husband and his Spanish advisers. Also, most of the leading merchants and gentry were firmly Protestant, and they were Elizabeth's strongest political supporters. In addition, one cannot see Elizabeth either embracing the religion that had called her a bastard (because it did not recognize Henry VIII's marriage to Anne Boleyn) or yielding any of her authority to foreign popes.

The country soon had its answer. The Acts of Settlement were enacted by Parliament in 1559. They consisted of two primary measures—the Act of Supremacy and the Act of Uniformity. The Act of Supremacy required all church and government officials to swear absolute loyalty to Elizabeth as Supreme Governor of the Church. A similar law had been passed by Henry VIII, but Henry's title had been Supreme Head of the Church. Elizabeth had no wish to make herself the final authority on matters of faith. She was far more interested in political rather than spiritual control. Nearly all the bishops, all of whom had been created by Mary, remained loyal to the pope, refused to take the oath, and were deprived of their offices. Ordinary priests, however, accepted the settlement. Only about two hundred of an estimated six thousand refused.

The Act of Uniformity

The Act of Uniformity was intended to make church services the same throughout the country. Elizabeth wanted to control the service so that it would not be too Catholic or too Protestant in character and thus would appeal to most of the people. The prayer book written during Edward VI's reign was reissued. It was not as extremely Protestant as the original and added language designed to appeal to Catholics. It succeeded in appealing to a wide range of Elizabeth's subjects. Only the most radical Protestants (the Puritans) and the most uncompromising Catholics (called "recusants") objected.

The Act of Uniformity also regulated what priests would wear and many other outward forms of religion. It also permitted priests to marry, unlike the Catholic church, and made church attendance compulsory. Every person was supposed to attend church in his or her home parish. Those who did not attend were fined.

A Step Toward Freedom

The Elizabethan Settlement concentrated on external worship instead of internal faith, whereas in other parts of Europe—especially in Spain—people suspected of having departed in the least from the established belief were tortured and burned at the stake. As long as people conformed outwardly, they could believe much as they wanted to.

The concept that differences in religious beliefs were acceptable was revolutionary. Throughout European history, any departure from the established system of belief laid down by the Catholic church had been "heresy," a crime against God. In dismissing some of the outward forms of religion as "trifles," Elizabeth came close to saying that a different form of worship was not necessarily evil. Complete freedom of religion still was a long way off, but the first step—an acknowledgment that people might still be good Christians although their beliefs differed slightly from those of their neighbors—had been taken.

Elizabeth's "trifles," the outward expressions of religion, still meant a great deal to the people. In their eagerness to erase Catholicism, the more extreme Protestants destroyed countless works of art considered symbols of "popery"—paintings, crucifixes, statues, tombs. A Puritan in Kent was delighted "to deface a monument of superstition, to put away a font-cast, coloured, gilded and pictures story-like with the seven popish sacraments . . . a great offence to all that are Christianly minded." [59]

The English may have lost relics and monuments through the Elizabethan Settlement, but they gained something more valuable in the long run—the Bible. The Bible had been translated into English under Henry VIII, who put copies in every church and then refused to permit ordinary people to read them. The word of God, he thought, was not to be debated, except by scholars. The English Bible had been banned by Mary, but Elizabeth, after great hesitation, permitted it, not only in churches, but also in homes.

Elizabeth's tolerant attitude toward religion differed vastly from the rest of Europe, where those that did not adhere to Roman Catholic beliefs were often tortured for heresy.

*The first English translation of the Bible is presented to Henry VIII. During
Elizabeth's reign the Bible would be made widely available.*

Sermonizing

Throughout Elizabeth's reign, thousands
learned to read so they could read the
Bible for themselves. Bible reading became
a family pastime. As more people read the
Bible, they discussed what it meant. Priests
were asked to explain certain passages. The
sermon became a feature of the Church of
England service. Some congregations
thought the service incomplete unless the
sermon lasted three hours.

The Elizabethan Settlement was one of
the most important aspects of Elizabeth's
reign. First, as Rowse wrote, it provided "the
maximum amount of unity for the English

people that could be combined with probably the greatest amount of liberty of opinion
that was possible under the circumstances."[60]
Second, it served as a great intellectual stim-
ulation. Permitted a range of beliefs and the
reading of the Bible, more people began to
think for themselves. Third, it provided a
system of belief and a moral guide—one
that set forth a general code of conduct
that depended on individual conscience
rather than on hard and fast rules—that
was in keeping with the independent,
broad-minded character of the English.

The Catholics, at first, could exist under this system. Later in the reign, however, threats from abroad ended the "calm
and quiet season."[61] These threats, which

included plots to kill Elizabeth and put Mary Queen of Scots on the throne, brought an increase in anti-Catholic laws. Then, in 1570, Pope Pius V, hoping to force a rebellion through which England would become Catholic once more, issued a decree excommunicating Elizabeth, declaring her deposed from the English throne, and calling on all faithful Catholics to rebel against her.

People's private beliefs were one thing to Elizabeth, but this was a direct challenge to her rule. Reaction was swift. The Catholic mass was forbidden, even in secret. Royal commissioners toured the country again, renewing the Oath of Supremacy. In addition, suspected Catholics were asked whether, if England were invaded by a Catholic country, they would fight for the queen. Catholics, if they answered this "Bloody Question" no, were traitors. Cuthbert Mayne, a priest who answered that all Catholics should fight, instead, for the invaders, was hanged.

The Jesuits in England

Catholic Europe increased the pressure on England in 1580 by sending into the country young English Catholics who had gone into exile and become Jesuits, members of the Society of Jesus. The mission of the Jesuits, whom Elizabeth's government outlawed, was to move secretly throughout the country—preaching, distributing Catholic literature, and urging rebellion. The government went

---

A Puritan Lady's Day

Religion was a vital part of every day's activities to the Puritans, as shown by this excerpt from the Diary of Lady Margaret Hoby, *a Yorkshire woman. It is found in* Elizabethan People: State and Society.

"In the morning after private prayers and order taken for dinner I wrote some notes in my Testament till 10 o'clock; then I went to walk and, after I returned home, I prayed privately, read a chapter of the Bible, and wrought [embroidered] till dinner time. After, I walked awhile with Mr. Rhodes [her chaplain] and then I wrought and did some good things about the house till 4. Then I wrote out the sermon into my book preached the day before and, when I had again gone about in the house and given order for supper and other things, I returned to examination and prayer. Then I walked till supper time and, after catechising [studying scripture], meditated awhile of that I had heard, with mourning to God for pardon both of my omission and commission wherein I found myself guilty, I went to bed."

When Pope Pius V excommunicated Elizabeth in 1570, urging Catholics to rebel against her, Elizabeth clamped down on Catholicism, banning the traditional mass.

tions should be directed toward God. Each person, the Puritans believed, could grow nearer to God by living as sober and pious a life as possible.

Consequently, Puritans lived strict, grim lives. Not only did they disapprove of images in churches, but they also wished to eliminate most holidays, including Christmas. Dancing, card playing, and sports of any kind were thought to be evil. The Puritans' recreation was praying, fasting, reading religious texts, and listening to sermons.

The Puritans not only lived this way, they also wanted everyone else to. No wonder Elizabeth hated them!

John Whitgift, Archbishop of Canterbury in the 1580s, was ordered by the queen to limit the efforts of the Puritans to reform the Church of England according to their

John Calvin led the Puritan movement. Elizabeth disliked the joyless Puritans and forced them to accept the English prayer book.

all out to stop them. Catholics were heavily fined and their lands were taken. Jesuits were hunted down and executed for treason. Still, fewer people were executed for their religion in thirty years of Elizabeth's reign than in the last three years of her sister's.

The vast majority of Catholics remained loyal to Elizabeth. The attempted invasion by Spain in 1588 depended on England's Catholics rising up against their queen. This would have been most unlikely. They were Englishmen first, Catholics second.

At the other end of the religious scale were the Puritans. Though they did not pose the same threat as the Catholics, Elizabeth liked them even less. The Puritan movement began when some Protestant exiles during Mary's reign settled in Geneva, Switzerland, and came under the influence of John Calvin. They believed that all aspects of life should center around the church and that all public and private ac-

A Puritan Sermon

The Puritans were convinced that most of the world around them was evil and would be condemned to hell. This was reflected in their sermons, such as this excerpt of one by Henry Smith. It is found in Elizabethan People: State and Society.

"If there be any hell in this world, they which feel the Worme of conscience gnaw upon their hearts, may truly say, that they have felt the torments of hell. Who can expresse that man's horror but himselfe? Sorrowes are met in his soule at a feast: and fear, thought, and anguish divide his soule between them. All the furies of hell leap upon his heart like a stag. Thought calleth to Fear; Fear whistleth to Horrour; Horrour beckoneth to Despair, and saith, Come and help me to torment the sinner: One saith, that she cometh from this sinne, and another saith, that she cometh from that sinne: so he goeth thorow [through] a thousand deaths, and cannot die. Irons are laid upon his body like a prisoner. All his lights are put out at once: he hath no soul fit to be comforted. Thus he lies upon the racke, and saith that he beares the world upon his shoulders, and that no man suffereth that which he suffereth. So let him lye (saith God) without ease, until he confesse and repent, and call for mercie. This is the godly way which the Serpent said would make you Gods, and made him a Devill."

A Puritan sermon. Puritans believed that the world around them was evil, and also believed in converting others to their faith.

Elizabeth outlawed the Jesuits, whose main goal was to incite rebellion among England's Catholics. In defiance of the law, Jesuits continued to work secretly in England.

own views. He did so by forcing Puritan clergymen to accept the Church of England prayer book as containing nothing "contrary to the word of the Lord." If they refused, they were removed and fined. He also punished Puritan writers and closed down the printers who published their works.

Whitgift was successful. The Puritan movement was suppressed for the time being. However, it was so popular among the middle class, including the leading merchants, that it would grow even stronger after Elizabeth's death. The Puritans gained complete control of England during the next century, in fact, but did not hold it long. One of the great accomplishments of Elizabeth was that, by acting to limit the power of both the Catholics and the Puritans, she gave the Church of England—created under her father and given substance under her brother—time to grow strong enough to survive.

Chapter

6 The Nation at Play

The people of the Elizabethan Era had a zest for living. They worked hard, and they played just as hard as they worked. Their lives were crude, rough, often violent, and so were their pastimes.

In earlier centuries, virtually the only physical activity for men had been war. Sports had been a training for battle. The Elizabethan gentleman viewed sports instead as pleasant, but important, pastimes, and people of all classes found them sources of amusement. Roger Ascham, Elizabeth's tutor while she was a young lady, urged young men

to ride comely, to run fair at the tilt or ring [trying to hit a target with a lance while on horseback], to play at all weapons, to shoot fair in bow, or surely in gun; to vault lustily, to run, to leap, to wrestle, to swim; to dance comely, to sing, and play of instruments cunningly; to hawk, to hunt, to play at tennis, and all pastimes generally which be joined with labour, used in open place, and on the day light, containing either some fit exercise for war, or some pleasant pastime for peace.[62]

An upper-class lady watches noblemen hunt deer. Hunting was the most popular sport for all classes.

Sport for a Gentleman

In Lord Herbert of Cherbury's (1583–1648) autobiography, he gives his opinion on which sort of pastimes are fit for gentlemen and which are not. This passage is from Elizabethan People: State and Society.

"It will be fit for a gentleman also to learn to swim, unless he be given to cramps and convulsions; howbeit, I must confes, in my own particular, that I cannot swim; for, as I was once in danger of drowning, by learning to swim, my mother, upon her blessing, charged me never to learn swimming, telling me further, that she had heard of more drowned than saved by it; which reason, though it did not prevail with me, yet her commandment did. It will be good also for a gentleman to learn to leap, wrestle, and vault on horseback; they being all of them qualities of great use. I do much approve likewise of shooting in the long-bow, as being both an healthful exercise and useful for the wars, notwithstanding all that our firemen [gunners] speak against it; for, bring an hundred archers against so many musqueteers, I say if the archer comes within his distance, he will not only make two shoots, but two hits for one. The exercises I do not approve of are riding of running horses, there being much cheating in that kind; neither do I see why a brave man should delight in a creature whose chief use is to help him to run away. . . . The exercises I wholly condemn, are dicing and carding, especially if you play for any great sum of money, or spend any time in them; or use to come to meetings in dicing-houses where cheaters meet and cozen [cheat] young gentlemen of all of their money."

Hunting was the most popular sport for all classes. England was still very rural and mostly open. Deer hunting was the favorite sport of the upper classes, as it had been for centuries. Common people were forbidden by law to hunt deer, and the poor man who killed one to feed his family could be hanged. Great nobles hunted on their own lands and sometimes kept deer parks, sections of forest set aside specifically for raising and hunting deer. In the chase, deer were flushed from hiding with packs of dogs and then pursued on horseback. When, at last, the deer fell exhausted, the first hunter to reach it would kill it by slitting its throat.

Another method of deer hunting was the drive. Servants, beating the bushes with sticks and making loud noises, drove the deer toward the edge of a wood or a clearing where hunters waited with bows and arrows. This was a sport for the less adventuresome and for those who might have considered racing around the countryside on horseback a bit vulgar:

A sport for noble peers, a sport for
  gentle bloods,
The pain I leave for servants such as
  beat the bushy woods.[63]

Elizabeth enjoyed this form of hunting as she grew older, but still loved the thrill of the chase. At age sixty-seven, she still could occasionally be found hunting on horseback.

Ordinary people enjoyed hunting, too. They were free to hunt the foxes, badgers, squirrels, otters, and hares that could be found throughout the countryside. "Coursing" the hares was extremely popular. Hares were captured and then given a twelve-yard head start over a pack of greyhounds. The object was to see who had the fastest dogs.

Falconry and Hawking

Game birds, such as quail, pheasant, and grouse, were plentiful, and the favorite way of hunting them was with falcons or hawks. Like deer hunting, falconry and hawking were sports for the wealthy. Birds were very expensive. Walter Raleigh once wrote to Robert Cecil, Lord Burghley's son, "If you will be so bountiful to give another falcon, I will provide you a running gelding (a horse)."[64] Falcons hunted by soaring far above their masters, then diving in for the kill when dogs flushed game birds from hiding.

Fishing appealed to those who enjoyed a less active, more peaceful pastime. Many rivers were full of salmon. Some towns farmed nearby streams, stretching nets across them to trap the fish. Individuals preferred "angling," fishing with hook and line. Anglers either used "still fishing," dropping baited hooks into the water, or "fly fishing," tying feathers onto hooks to make them look like insects and then casting them over the water. Then, as now, fishing was a way to get away from it all. Elizabethan Richard Carew wrote:

I wait not at the lawyers' gates,
  Nor shoulder climbers down the stairs;

Queen Elizabeth enjoyed falconry and hawking, both favorite pastimes of the English nobility during the Elizabethan Era.

A bull is set upon by a lion and powerful dogs in the popular blood sport of animal-baiting.

I vault not manhood by debates,
I envy not the miser's fears:
But mean in state and calm in sprite,
My full fish-pond is my delight.[65]

Horse racing became popular in England under Henry VIII and continued under Elizabeth. In her reign, books on horse breeding and training were published. Not only the nobles but also the gentry raced horses. Many towns built tracks and organized series of races to which owners brought their horses. Although owning and racing horses were only for the wealthy, people of the towns flocked to see and bet on the races, making it one of England's few spectator sports.

Other spectator sports included the violent blood sports such as bear-baiting, bull-baiting, and cockfighting. The animals to be baited—bears, bulls, and sometimes even lions or apes—would be held by a length of chain to a stake, and dogs—bulldogs or mastiffs—would be set loose on them. The dogs would rush in and try to seize the larger animals in their strong jaws before they could be clawed, gored, or swatted away. The dogs won if the larger animal was killed. They lost if so many of them were disabled that the rest refused to attack.

Cockfighting was another popular sport. Roosters were fitted with sharp blades on each foot and put into a pit to fight to the death. Fighting cocks, like falcons, were expensive. It took a well-to-do man (cockfighting seems to have been an all-male pastime) to own cocks, but men of all classes came to see and bet on the fights.

The Appeal of Violence

The blood sports, thought by most people today to be too gruesome, cruel, and violent, had great appeal for the Elizabethans. Large crowds of both men and women of all classes flocked to see baiting, and Elizabeth frequently used it to entertain visiting ambassadors. "The average

Elizabethan," wrote historian M. St. Clair Byrne, "was not sensitive to the spectacle of physical suffering, either in human beings or in animals."[66]

Team sports gained in popularity during Elizabeth's reign, and they were just as rough and violent as those involving animals. The two most played by common men (but not women) were hurling and football.

Both were ball games. Hurling was like a combination of hockey and polo. Some players were on foot; others, on horseback. The object of the game was to strike a ball so that it went over the opponents' goal. The ball was struck toward the goal by a stick or club. Hurling was more organized in towns, with up to thirty men on a side and definite goals to cross. Country hurling might match the entire adult male populations of two villages, and the goals might be three or four miles apart.

Football (not an ancestor of American football, despite the similarities) got its name not because the ball was kicked but because all the players went on foot. The ball was carried, and whoever carried it became a target for tacklers. As in hurling, the "field" often was the countryside between two villages. Football was incredibly violent, with few or no rules. John Stubbes wrote:

> Doth not everyone lie in wait for his adversary, seeking to overthrow him and to pitch him on the nose, though it be upon hard stones, in ditch or dale, in valley or hill, or what place soever it be, he careth not, so he have him down? And he that can serve the most of this fashion, he is counted the only fellow . . . so that by this means sometimes their necks are broken, sometimes their backs, sometimes their legs, sometimes their arms; sometime one part thrust out of joint, sometime another; sometime the noses gush out with blood, sometime their eyes start out.[67]

The main reason that Stubbes, a Puritan, disliked football was that it was played on Sunday, when the Puritans thought everyone should be either in church or in spiritual meditation. He wrote, "Any exercise which withdraweth us from godliness, either upon the sabbath or any other day, is wicked and to be forbidden."[68]

The government objected to it also, but only because it took time away from archery. The government felt men were spending too much time playing football and too little practicing with bow and arrow. The longbow had been England's chief weapon of war for two hundred years, and both Henry VIII and Elizabeth

The government encouraged the sport of archery because the longbow was the main weapon used in war.

made archery practice mandatory for all able-bodied villagers.

Fencing

Fencing, enjoyed by the nobles, was another sport left over from warfare. The English had always preferred the broadsword and buckler (a small, round shield), but the long, slim rapier became fashionable during the Elizabethan Era, largely because it was more elegant to wear. Playwright Henry Porter lamented:

> Sword and buckler fight begin to grow out of use. I am sorry for it. I shall

An Elizabethan Christmas

Christmas was the chief holiday for all Elizabethans, except for the Puritans. Nicholas Breton, in his Fantastickes, *gives this description. It is found in* The Horizon Book of the Elizabethan World *by Lacey Baldwin Smith.*

"It is now Christmas, and not a cup of drink must pass without a carol; the beast, fowl, and fish come to general execution; and the corn is ground to dust for the bakehouse, and the pastry. Cards and dice purge many a purse, and the youth show their agility in shoeing of the wild mare. Now 'Good cheer' and 'Welcome,' and 'God be with you,' and 'I thank you,' and 'Against the new year,' provide for the presents. The Lord of Misrule is no mean man for his time, and the guests of the high table must lack no wine. The lusty bloods must look about them like men, and piping and dancing puts away much melancholy. Stolen venison is sweet, and a fat coney is worth money. Pit-falls are now set for small birds, and a woodcock hangs himself in gin. A good fire heats all the house, and a full alms-basket makes the beggars prayers. The masquers and mummers make the merry sport; but if they lose their money, their drum goes dead. Swearers and swaggerers are sent away to the ale-house, and unruly wenches to in danger of judgment. Musicians now make their instruments speak out, and a good song is worth the hearing. In sum, it is a holy time, a duty in Christians for the remembrance of Christ, and custom among friends for the maintenance of good fellowship. In brief, I thus conclude of it: I hold it a memory of the Heaven's love and the world's peace, the mirth of the honest, and the meeting of the friendly."

danced at dawn on Easter Sunday, not realizing the practice dated back to sun worshipping. In one country parish, a bull was sacrificed to a patron saint.

The Church-Ale

Rural English churches were places for fun as well as for faith. When churches needed new roofs or windows, the money was usually raised through church-ales. Nearby farmers donated malt, and a very strong ale was brewed and sold to people who came from miles around to the church to buy it. The more one drank, the greater the gift to God. One writer said:

Townspeople dance in an Elizabethan courtyard. Dancing was popular with everyone except the Puritans.

never see good manhood again. If it be once gone, this poking fight with rapier and dagger will come up. Then the tall man will be spitted like a cat or a rabbit.[69]

On the more refined side, dancing was popular with everyone except, of course, the Puritans, who believed it was sinful. Elizabeth was passionately fond of dancing. She once asked a French ambassador who was the better dancer, herself or Mary Queen of Scots? The ambassador replied that Mary "danced not so high and disposedly as she did."[70]

The calendar was full of festivals and feasts for all classes. Almost all were church holidays, although some originated in pre-Christian customs. The use of mistletoe and a Yule log went back thousands of years. In some areas, people

Street revelers frolic during Christmastime. Largely because of the temperament of their ruler, Elizabethans enjoyed parties and celebration.

Then when . . . this duff cap [ale] . . . is set abroach, well is he that can get the soonest to it and spend the most at it; for he that sitteth the closest to it and spends the most at it, he is counted the godliest man of all the rest.[71]

Christmas was the greatest of all festivals. Feasting and dancing lasted twelve days—from Christmas Eve to Twelfth Night. Masques, plays, and feasts were held each night at court and in the houses of the nobles and gentry. Even in the houses of the common people, it was a time for merrymaking and as rich food as was affordable, including the traditional Christmas dishes of roast goose, plum pudding, and "wassail," a spiced wine. Everyone exchanged gifts on New Year's Day. One year, Leicester gave Elizabeth a "very fair jewel of gold, being a clock fully furnished with small diamonds and an apple of gold enameled green and russet."[72] Even the poorest people exchanged gifts, often no more than an apple or an orange.

The sports and pastimes of Elizabethan England were challenged in the next century by the Puritans. When the Puritan Parliament ruled England during the Commonwealth (1647–1660), Christmas and most other holidays were abolished. Games and plays were forbidden. But the spirit of the Elizabethan Era proved to be too strong, and the country gladly welcomed back both its king and its customs.

7 Elizabethan Drama

The Elizabethan Age, particularly the last twenty years of Elizabeth's reign, was marked by a great increase in artistic expression. Three key ingredients—internal peace, increased wealth, and a queen who loved the arts—combined to transform the impulses of the Italian Renaissance (Europe's "rebirth" of culture) into something uniquely English.

Nowhere was this more true than in drama. The Elizabethan theater mirrored its times. It was poetic, crude, patriotic, emotional, and very class-conscious. Drama was the first and most important cultural export of England.

The drama that flourished in the last two decades of the sixteenth century was not yet considered literature. Plays were entertainment, meant to be performed rather than read. Educated persons thought playwrights inferior to poets—craftsmen instead of artists. It was not until the year of William Shakespeare's death (1616) that a book of his plays was published.

Elizabethan drama had its roots in the medieval church. Because the church service was in Latin, which most people could not understand, priests taught their congregations stories from the Bible by enacting them. At first, this was done in front of the altars inside churches. As the plays grew more elaborate and more people wanted to see them, they were moved to a platform outside the church. When there were not enough priests to fill all the roles, citizens from the town were used.

Gradually, these "mystery" plays on biblical themes were taken over by the people, usually by members of craft guilds, and became less connected with the church. Various parts of a play—the creation, Noah's

The earliest forms of English drama were called mystery plays. They revolved around Biblical themes and were often performed on portable stages.

A Love Song

Music and singing played a major role in Elizabethan England. All cultured persons were expected to be able to play an instrument or, at the very least, to be able to sing. This love song by Ben Jonson is found in The Horizon Book of the Elizabethan World *by Lacey Baldwin Smith.*

Come, my Celia, let us prove,
While we can, the sports of love;
Time will not be ours for ever,
He, at length, our good will sever.
Spend not then his gifts in vain:
Suns that set may rise again;
But if once we lose this light,
Tis with us perpetual night.
Why should we defer our joys?
Fame and rumour are but toys.
Cannot we delude the eyes
Of a few poor household spies?
Or his easier ears beguile,
Thus removéd by our wile?
'Tis no sin love's fruits to steal,
But the sweet thefts to reveal;
To be taken, to be seen.
These have crimes accounted been.

flood, the crucifixion of Jesus—were performed on portable stages or on large wagons in different areas of the town.

As the townspeople took over production of the plays, the plays changed in character. They became more entertaining in addition to being informative. Some stories remained solemn, but others became comedies. For example, Noah's wife, hardly mentioned in the Bible, was made a nagging, domineering woman bossing her meek husband. Satan, instead of being totally evil, became a mischievous rogue whose antics onstage brought laughter to the crowd. This was the forerunner of the often bawdy humor in Elizabethan plays.

The Renaissance Influence

English drama changed toward the end of the 1400s when the Tudors came to the throne. Two types of plays were developed, one for the educated and upper classes and the other for the common people. The main influence on drama for the educated was the Renaissance. Scholars and people of the upper classes, who were more exposed to the Renaissance influence from other countries, wanted to go back to the classical plays of ancient Greece and Rome.

Classical drama became a significant part of education. Schools and universities required students to perform in plays to teach them speech, diction, and self-confidence. The plays, performed in Latin or Greek, were either those by the classic playwrights, such as Euripides or Seneca, or plays written in the ancient manner. Student actors also performed these plays, in English, for members of the nobility in the great halls of their houses.

Drama for the common people was greatly influenced by the establishment of the Protestant Church of England. The ancient mystery plays were considered part of the old Catholic tradition and were mostly abandoned. The new fashion was the "morality" play. These were still religious in character, but they attempted, instead of telling a Bible story, to teach people how

A passion play (a play whose theme revolved around the events of the Biblical passion of Christ) is performed in the center of London.

to live a proper life. Characters did not represent people, but human qualities, such as Knowledge, Beauty, and Truth. Audiences, however, still wanted to be entertained, and the most popular character of the morality plays was Vice, the mischievous Satan of the mystery plays under a different name.

A third major influence on early Tudor drama was the War of the Roses. Before the Tudors, the only real professional actors were those employed by great nobles for household entertainment. The deaths of so many nobles in the war reduced the demand for actors. This, combined with the change toward the more scholarly, classical plays, threw many actors out of work. Many of them banded together to form troupes—touring companies of actors who went from town to town giving plays. These, wrote drama historian G. B. Harrison, "were really the founders of the acting profession."[73]

The Acting Tradition

Wandering entertainers had been around for centuries. Jugglers, acrobats, and tightrope walkers were to be seen at every village fair and in towns on market days. The difference in early Tudor times was that the emphasis was on plays.

In the first half of the sixteenth century, actors had generally bad reputations. They were considered disreputable—little better than beggars or thieves. Indeed, the actors sometimes were thieves. While some members of a touring company held the attention of the audience, others might move through the crowd picking pockets. When not performing, some actors might set up crooked gambling games, cheating the townspeople out of their money.

The touring companies were not large, usually fewer than ten actors. They traveled in wagons, sleeping in or under them when between towns. There were almost no women actors; women's parts were played by young boys. Sometimes actors were paid a fee by a city for providing entertainment on some special occasion. Most of the time they lived on the money—usually a penny a person—they collected from their audiences.

Plays were usually performed in the courtyards of inns. The stage consisted of planks laid across a raised framework. Even today, actors speak of being onstage as "treading the boards." The stage was placed next to the inn's door, and the door was covered with a curtain through which the actors made entrances and exits. The audience thus surrounded the stage on three sides.

Because everything had to fit into wagons and then be moved on- and offstage through the inn door, there was very little scenery. A gilded chair had to represent an entire throne room. A couple of small trees in pots became a whole forest.

Costumes were a different matter. Elizabethan playgoers loved elaborate costumes, and this was the most expensive part of a touring company's gear. Actors in small roles might get by dressed in contemporary clothes, but the major characters, who were supposed to be biblical characters, or Roman soldiers, or Persian princes, were expected to look the part.

Touring companies still performed the old mystery and morality plays, but they also wrote plays of their own. The few that have survived seem poorly written when compared with later works. These earlier, anonymous playwrights entertained their audiences with lewd or coarse humor—as in the farce that featured characters with names like Madge Mumblecrust—or with violent action that left the stage littered with supposedly dead bodies.

A traveling drama troupe performs in the courtyard of a London inn. Such troupes became popular during Elizabeth's time.

The Elizabethan love of drama fostered the building of the first theaters.
Although sets remained plain, actors often wore elaborate costumes.

The Companies

As Elizabeth's reign went on, it became harder and harder for troupes to get permission to perform in towns. The more reputable companies sought the sponsorship and protection of nobles who would vouch for their honesty and professionalism. Many nobles, such as Leicester and the queen herself, sponsored companies. The Poor Laws of 1572, which made it a criminal offense to be a vagabond, limited the number of acting companies and required them to be licensed by the government. The companies already being sponsored by nobles were given licenses.

The gaining of legal status was an important step for the acting profession. Now, the informal protection they had from their sponsors was backed by law. This was very useful because of the increasing hostility of city officials to plays and actors.

Burbage's Theatre

Elizabethan drama took its most important step in 1576, when James Burbage built "The Theatre," the first building in England devoted to plays. Burbage, an actor in Leicester's company and a former carpenter, thought it would be a good investment in addition to giving the company a place to perform. Because London officials did not want the building inside the city, he built The Theatre in the suburb of Shoreditch, outside the council's control. With permanent buildings, drama became "theater"—not merely actors saying lines, but new elements of staging, costumes, and sound effects.

The Theatre and later buildings, such as the Rose and the famous Globe, were built much like the courtyards the actors were used to. The building was circular, with the stage extending out so that the audience almost surrounded it. Scenery was still limited, but special effects were possible. Actors could pop up onto the stage through trapdoors or be lowered onto the stage from a room above known as "heaven." At the rear of the stage were two doors for both scenery and actors. Backstage were rooms for storage, the "tiring room" (where the actors got attired, or dressed), and the green room, where they waited for their cues to go onstage.

The Wicked Theater

The upright merchants of London frowned on the theater since it tended to distract people from work and worship. This passage is from an act of the City of London council in 1574. It is found in The Horizon Book of the Elizabethan World.

"Sundry great disorders and inconveniences have been found to ensue to this city by the inordinate haunting of great multitudes of people, especially youth, to plays, interludes, and shows—namely, occasion of frays and quarrels; evil practices of incontinency in great inns have chambers and secret places adjoining to their open stages and galleries; inveigling and alluring of maids, specially orphans and good citizens' children under age, to privy and unmeet contacts; the publishing of unchaste, uncomely, and unshamefast speeches and doings; withdrawing of the queen's majesty's subjects from divine service on Sundays and holidays, at which times such plays were chiefly used; unthrifty waste of the money of the poor and found persons; sundry robberies by picking and cutting of purses; uttering of popular, busy, and seditious matters; and many other corruptions of youth and other enormities—besides that also sundry slaughters and mayhemings of the queen's subjects have happened by ruins of scaffolds, frames, and stages, and by engines, weapons, and powder used in plays."

Actors perform a Shakespearean play on a stage that is characteristic of the Elizabethan Era. The stage extends into the audience-seating area.

The price of admission was a penny, which entitled one to stand on the ground around the stage. These poorest and often most boisterous playgoers were looked down on by the more well-to-do in the audience, who called them "groundlings." Entrance to the lowest of three galleries circling the stage cost another penny, and the price grew greater the higher one sat. The highest gallery might have private rooms, but the most expensive seats were those on the stage itself. Those who sat there often disturbed the performances, talking, playing cards, or showing off new clothes.

The Theatre was an immediate success, popular with both the upper classes and the lower. Middle-class merchants, mostly Puritans, disliked plays, but their apprentices often sneaked away from work to watch them. The audience was mostly male. Going to a public theater, even if escorted by a husband or male relative, was not considered respectable for a woman. Only prostitutes and women of the lowest classes went to plays by themselves. Upper-class women and the greatest nobles enjoyed plays, but they had the actors come to them and perform in private halls.

The Globe

The most famous of all the Elizabethan theaters was the Globe. In 1594, James Burbage's lease on the land on which The Theatre stood had run out, and the landlord wanted to raise the rent. The dispute dragged on for years. Finally, instead of paying, Burbage tore the building down, transported the lumber across the River Thames to Southwark, and built the Globe. The new theater was occupied by the newly formed Lord Chamberlain's Players, founded by Elizabeth's cousin, Lord Hundson. This most famous of Elizabethan companies included not only Shakespeare but also James Burbage's son, Richard, considered the best actor of the time.

The Globe opened to the public in 1599 with Shakespeare's *Henry V*, and some drama historians believe Shakespeare himself played the part of Chorus, saying:

But pardon gentles all,
The flat unraisèd spirits that hath

dared

On this unworthy scaffold to bring
    forth
so great an object. Can this cockpit
    hold
The vasty [vast] fields of France? Or
    may we cram
Within this wooden O the very casques
    [helmets]
That did affright the air at [the Battle
    of] Agincourt?[74]

Equally as important in the development of Elizabethan drama as permanent theaters was the improvement in quality of the plays performed there. The old plays that satisfied patrons at inns around the country were not enough for a more sophisticated London audience. New and better plays were demanded, plays that would appeal both to the groundlings and to those who enjoyed classical drama. They were provided by a series of college-trained playwrights known as the "University Wits." "In their hands," wrote drama historian G. B. Harrison, "drama ceased to be doggerel [crudely written] and became literature."[75]

James Burbage's son, Richard (pictured), is considered the finest of the Elizabethan actors. He performed with Shakespeare in the most famous of the Elizabethan acting companies.

The earliest of the University Wits was John Lyly, whose *Campaspe* was first performed in 1584. *Campaspe* was the first truly

The Globe Theatre is the most well-known of Elizabethan theaters. Built by James Burbage with the remnants of The Theatre, the Globe opened in 1599 with Shakespeare's Henry V.

Elizabethan play. It was highly popular despite depending on verbal wit rather than slapstick comedy or violent action. A year later, Thomas Kyd's *Spanish Tragedy* was staged. It was such a hit that it would be revived every now and then for more than fifty years.

Other highly popular authors included Christopher Marlowe, Robert Greene, and Thomas Nashe. Marlowe's first play, *Tamburlaine*, was staged in 1587, and he quickly became the most popular playwright in England. His other notable works were *Faustus* and *The Jew of Malta*. Marlowe, wrote A. L. Rowse, "was the first to marry splendid verse to the stage, he was the creator of the 'mighty line,' the blank verse that was to be its chief vehicle. He was the originator, the pioneer."[76]

Shakespeare

Marlowe died young, killed in a tavern fight in 1593 at the age of twenty-nine. His successor, however, had already arrived in the person of William Shakespeare, who had decided on drama as his career after seeing the Queen's Players visit his hometown of Stratford-on-Avon in 1587.

When Marlowe died, Shakespeare was already well known in London for his three-part *Henry VI*, written in 1592. In 1594, *Love's Labour's Lost* and *Romeo and Juliet* were performed and he became famous as the outstanding playwright of the time. Before Elizabeth's reign was over, Shakespeare staged such timeless masterpieces as *Richard II, Julius Caesar, Henry V,* and *Hamlet*.

In writing plays to appeal to a mass audience, many of the established rules of classical Greek drama as established by the philosopher Aristotle were ignored. One

rule, for instance, was that all the action had to be in a single place with no change of scene. Also, the period covered in a play was supposed to be the same time it took to act it. In other words, a three-hour play was to cover only the events of a single, three-hour period. Elizabethan audiences found such plays dull. Spanish playwright Lope de Vega lamented, "The audience stays away when he [the playwright] composes in accordance with all these excellent principles [Aristotle's rules]. . . . The audience pays for plays, and so the taste of the audience must be followed."[77] A play's appeal to large numbers of ticket buyers became more important than its artistic merit.

William Shakespeare was a playwright for all time. He was so successful at writing plays that appealed to everyone that modern day theatergoers still enjoy his plays.

Shakespeare on Acting

William Shakespeare gave his view of what was required of Elizabethan actors in this speech from Hamlet *by the title character. It is found in* Elizabethan People: State and Society.

"Be not too tame neither, but let your own discretion be your tutor. Suit the action to the word, the word to the action; with this special observance, that you o'erstep not the modesty of nature; for anything so o'erdone is from the purpose of playing, whose end, both at the first and now, was and is to hold as 'twere the mirror up to nature; to show virtue her own feature, scorn her own image, and the very age and body of the time his form and pressure. Now, this overdone or come tardy off, though it makes the unskillful laugh, cannot but make the judicious grieve; the censure of the which one must, in your allowance, o'erweigh a whole theatre of others. Oh, there be players that I have seen play—and heard others praise, and that highly—not to speak it profanely, that, neither having th' accent of Christians, nor the gait of Christian, pagan, nor man, have so strutted and bellowed that I have thought some of Nature's journeymen had made men, and not made them well, they imitated humanity so abominably."

The plays reflected the enthusiasm of the times. The audience wanted plenty of action—bloody swordfights, rib-tickling humor—and playwrights had to provide it. As a result, Elizabethan acting was highly emotional and full of extravagant gestures. Love scenes and death scenes were played to stir desire or bring tears.

The golden age of Elizabethan drama did not long outlive the queen herself. Younger playwrights, like Ben Jonson, returned to the classical forms of drama with their strict rules. Playwrights began to ignore the tastes of the groundlings and wrote what they thought would appeal to the upper classes. Smaller, private theaters became fashionable. Elizabethan drama survived, however, as English actors carried it throughout Europe. And the publication of Shakespeare's plays saved them for future, more appreciative generations.

8 Literature and the Visual Arts

Drama was by no means the only area in which the fine arts advanced during the Elizabethan Age. Although painting and sculpture had been so stifled by religious change that they would not revive until later centuries, literature, music, and architecture captured and reflected the spirit of Elizabethan life and had great influence throughout Europe.

Poetry and essays were the chief forms of literature in Elizabethan England. Their contributions, although not as spectacular as that of drama, were just as important. They went a long way toward standardizing the English language and earning it a certain respect.

Throughout much of history, English had been the language of the common people only. The nobility, many of whom held land both in England and France, spoke French. Not until 1327 did England have a king—Edward III—who even spoke English. One observer wrote during the Elizabethan Age that English had "been accounted barbarous much more than it now is—before it was enriched and amplified by sundry books, in manner of all arts, translated out of Latin and other tongues."[78]

As a result of the growth of literature, the version of English written and spoken within sixty miles of London—an area that included the major universities of Oxford and Cambridge—began to be considered "standard" English. The many regional dialects remained, but the time was ending when people from north and south might not understand one another. Spelling, also, was beginning to be simplified and made more uniform, such as "man" instead of "manne."

English literature thus got its start in the Elizabethan Age. Rowse wrote, "Where before the Elizabethans, there was no continuous English literature, after them it flourished, rich, mature and full. They started it."[79]

The most important figures in Elizabethan literature were Marlowe, Shakespeare, Edmund Spenser, Philip Sidney, and Francis Bacon. The quality of their works helped make all classes of Englishmen proud of their language and provided a foundation on which future English and American writers would build.

Philip Sidney

Sidney, in addition to being a poet, was famous as a soldier and a statesman. A nephew of Leicester, he was close to the queen and very much at home at court. His *Astrophel and Stella* was the first series

Edmund Spenser

Philip Sidney contributed much to the modern idea of poetry, including developing the terms lyrical, stanza, couplet, *and* octave.

of sonnets (a type of poem containing fourteen lines) in English. It became very popular and led to an outburst of sonnet writing, including those by Shakespeare.

Sidney's other outstanding contribution was in the mechanics of poetry and its standing among literary forms. Perhaps because of a growing antagonism toward poetry from the Puritans, Sidney wrote *An Apology for Poetry*. In this book, Sidney not only defended poetry as superior to other literature, but also created many of the terms by which poetry is written, studied, and criticized—terms such as *lyrical, stanza, couplet,* and *octave*.

Spenser was even more popular than Sidney because his poems appealed to the ordinary reader as well as to the highly educated. His most important work was *The Faerie Queene*, a huge (six volumes) epic dedicated to Elizabeth herself in which she is given the name "Gloriana." In *The Faerie Queene*, Spenser was attempting to raise the reputation of English poetry by writing a work to rival the very popular *Orlando Furioso* by the Italian Ludovico Ariosto. He succeeded not only in composing a masterpiece but also in creating a work that increased England's national pride. The story of *The Faerie Queene* is the story of the Elizabethan Age. Its heroes, heroines, and their deeds—although given different names in the poem—were recognizable to readers. The work also was a landmark in poetry because in it Spenser first used the nine-line stanza that is still known today as "Spenserian."

Marlowe and Shakespeare did not set out, as did Sidney and Spenser, to increase the reputation of English poetry. They did so as a result of the beauty of their language and the contributions they made toward English vocabulary. Before the Elizabethan Age, English contained far fewer words than other European languages. This limited the ways in which a poet or playwright might express ideas. Both Marlowe and Shakespeare borrowed words from Greek, Latin, French, and Italian and made them part of English. Some of the best examples of these are words associated with plays, such as *drama, theater, prologue*, and *chorus*.

Music was much more important to the Elizabethans than were either drama or lit-

A Spenserian Sonnet

The fourteen-line sonnet was the most popular form of Elizabethan poetry. One estimate is that more than a million were written during the sixteenth century. This one by Edmund Spenser is found in The Horizon Book of the Elizabethan World.

Is it her nature or is it her will,
To be so cruel to an humbled foe?
If nature, then she may it mend with skill,
If will, then she at will may will forego.
But if her nature and her will be so,
That she will plague the man that loves her most:
And take delight t' increase a wretch's woe,
Then all her nature's goodly gifts are lost.
And that same glorious beauty's idle boast,
Is but a bait such wretches to beguile:
As being long in her love's tempest tossed,
She means at last to make her piteous spoil.
O fairest fair let never it be named,
That so fair beauty was so foully shamed.

Poet Edmund Spenser's works appealed to the average reader. He also invented the nine-line stanza.

A Richness of Language

William Shakespeare, the greatest writer in the history of England, and perhaps of the world, enriched the language as no other has done. This passage from his Henry VI, Part 2 *is found in* The Horizon Book of the Elizabethan World.

". . . Of comfort no man speak:
Let's talk of graves, of worms, and epitaphs;
Make dust our paper, and with rainy eyes
Write sorrow on the bosom of the earth;
Let's choose executors and talk of wills:
And yet not so—for what can we bequeath
Save our deposed bodies to the ground?
Our lands, our lives, and all are Bolingbroke's
   [Henry IV],
And nothing can we call our own by death,
And that small model of the barren earth
Which serves as paste and cover to our bones.
For God's sake, let us sit upon the ground
And tell sad stories of the death of kings:
How some have been depos'd, some slain in war,
Some haunted by the ghosts they have depos'd,
Some poisoned by their wives, some sleeping kill'd;
All murder'd: for within the hollow crown
That rounds the mortal temples of a king
Keeps Death his court, and there the antick sits,
Scoffing his state and grinning at his pomp;
Allowing him a breath, a little scene,
To monarchize, be fear'd, and kill with looks,
Infusing him with self and vain conceit
As if this flesh which walls about our life
Were brass impregnable; and humor'd thus
Comes at the last, and with a little pin
Bores through his castle wall, and farewell king!"

erature. Music had always been a part of everyday life throughout the country, whether it was performed before the nobility or at a village festival. The difference in the Elizabethan Age was that men and women of all classes were expected, instead of merely listening to music, to play an instrument or at least to sing in harmony. Thomas Morley, author of *Plaine and Easie Introduction to Practical Music* in 1597, wrote:

Supper being ended and the Music books, according to the custom, being brought to the table: the mistress of the house presented me with a part, earnestly requesting me to sing. But when after many excuses, I protested that I could not: every one began to wonder. Yea, some whispered to others, demanding how I was brought up.[80]

Indeed, the Elizabethans "were looked to by the whole of Europe as the most musical of civilized nations."[81] Other countries sought out English musicians to come teach them the English madrigal, a form of poetry set to music and sung by anywhere from three to eight voices. The madrigal had originated in Italy, but English madrigal singing was considered the best in the world by the time of Elizabeth's reign.

There were two types of madrigals. The first was the Italian, in which the words received as much attention as the music and in which the melody tended to be slower and more dramatic. The greatest composer of the Italian madrigal in English was Thomas Morley. In the English madrigal, the words were secondary to the music, which was sprightlier and more rhythmic,

The English were known throughout Europe for their exceptional musical ability. European noblemen and monarchs hired English tutors to teach their musicians the mechanics of the madrigal, a form of poetry set to music and sung by a number of voices.

Elizabethan music was known for its steady rhythm and its polyphony—multiple melodies weaving in and out of one another.

and featured multiple "voices," or melodies, weaving among one another. Thomas Weekes and John Wilby, both of whom had been Morley's students, were considered the masters of the English madrigal.

The English Madrigal

The characteristics of the English madrigal were the same that distinguished most non-religious Elizabethan music from that of the rest of Europe. First, it had a steady rhythm underneath the melody, probably from the influence of native folk dances. Second, Elizabethan music tended to be polyphonic—multiple melodies weaving around one another—rather than harmonic—a single melody with chords made up of notes sung or played simultaneously.

English instrumental music was famous as well. The most popular instrument was the virginal (a type of small piano). The best known keyboard composers were William Byrd—considered by modern au-

thorities the greatest of all Elizabethan composers—John Bull (best known as an organist), and Orlando Gibbons. An enormous amount of keyboard music was composed and published in England, and sold throughout Europe. The most important English contribution to keyboard music was the "variation," a work in which a main theme is established and then played in different, more complex ways.

The other popular instrument was the lute, an early form of guitar. Lute songs and vocal songs written to be accompanied by the lute were usually slower and more emotional than madrigals and often were for a solo singer. The leading composer of lute music, not only in England but also in all Europe, was John Dowland.

Church Music

Although much English music during the Elizabethan Age was secular, church music grew as well. The Puritans wanted to do away with music in church altogether, but part of the Religious Settlement of 1559 allowed "a modest and distinct song . . . that the same might be as plainly understood as if it were read without singing."[82] Before long, hundreds of hymns had been written, many of which still are sung today. The English love of music was too much for even the Puritans to overcome.

The leading composer of religious music was Byrd. Although a Catholic who legally should not have been allowed to write for the Church of England, his talent was so great that he was chief organist and composer for Elizabeth herself, who called him "a strong papist, but a good subject."[83] He was best known in his lifetime for his motets, religious songs that were not part of the mass (the songs used regularly as a standard part of the church service). He also secretly wrote three Catholic masses, published only after his death. Byrd's church music is still widely performed today, in both Protestant and Catholic churches.

Architecture is the most visible expression of Elizabethan art remaining today.

Evidence of the Elizabethans' passion for building can be seen in almost all towns and cities and throughout the countryside. It is yet another reflection of the peace and prosperity of the time.

Until Elizabeth's reign, there had been no English architects. Instead, there were master builders who copied designs from other countries—mostly Italy. England did not produce a unique style until Robert Smythson blended the Italian style with the medieval Gothic style that had dominated English building. When Smythson died in 1616, the inscription on his tomb was "architector."

Elizabeth did not share the enthusiasm for building. She had enough royal palaces and had no wish to spend money on others. Her chief subjects, however, tried to outdo one another in the extravagance of their houses. There were no finer homes in England—including Elizabeth's palaces—than Burghley's Theobalds or Leicester's Kenilworth. The upper gentry shared the building mania. It was not unusual for a gentleman to build himself into bankruptcy.

Wealthy Elizabethans tried to outdo each other in the elaborate design and decoration of their homes. Pictured is Kenilworth, Leicester's estate.

Architecture flourished in the cities and with the homes of the lesser gentry as well as with the great manor houses. The most distinctive expression of Elizabethan architecture was the "timbered" house. The wooden timbers, usually oak, used to frame the houses were built in patterns and left exposed on the outside. The spaces between the beams were filled in with plaster. The contrast of the dark beams and the white plaster is what most people think of as typical "Elizabethan" architecture.

The Manor House

There was also a distinctive Elizabethan style in the palaces of the very wealthy. It was based not on the classical Greek and Roman architecture or the ornate buildings of Renaissance Italy but instead on the traditional English Perpendicular style, which emphasized vertical lines. The distinguishing features of the Elizabethan manor house were a low, rather square shape with banks of high windows.

Architecture was the only visual art form that expanded in the Elizabethan Era. Both painting and sculpture declined in importance. Both had been closely tied to religion; and the new Protestantism, although it kept music, discouraged decoration. Many medieval statues, tombs, and shrines were torn down, and statues were specifically prohibited from Protestant churches. What little sculpture there was took the form of effigies (likenesses) or busts of prominent men and women on their tombs.

Painting, as well, suffered from the Protestant movement. Religious murals in churches were scraped off walls or whitewashed over. In the early years of Elizabeth's reign, most painting was mere decoration. It became fashionable in the interiors of houses to plaster stone walls and wooden ceilings and to paint them with colors and designs and even to paint walls to look like curtains.

The growth in painting, when it came, was in portraits. Before Elizabeth, only

The characteristic timbered house of the Elizabethan period reveals the way exterior wood was used to create patterns.

A portrait of Elizabeth by Nicholas Hilliard. Although painting was discouraged during Elizabeth's time, portraits gained in popularity especially after the queen hired Hilliard to paint her portrait.

rulers and their highest nobles had their portraits painted. With the rise of the gentry and the wealthy merchant class, more people looked on themselves as the founders of great families and wanted to leave likenesses for their descendants to admire.

The fashion in portraits went from the large, framed versions to the other extreme—miniatures. Elizabeth began the fashion, choosing Nicholas Hilliard, who specialized in miniatures, as the artist to paint her official portraits. Hilliard's miniatures were the finest paintings produced by Elizabethan England.

The Elizabethans were very conscious of their status in society. They wanted their portraits to show them not as they were, but as how they wanted to be. Elizabeth's own portraits illustrate this best. She is portrayed as a lofty, remote symbol of majesty, not as a woman of flesh and blood. The Elizabethans did not want realism. One gentleman, John Davies, wrote this poem to painter Rowland Lockley:

As nature made, so thou dost make my face
Yet with a better, and a worser, grace:
With better, since thy work hath glory got,
With worse, since thou giv'st life that moves it not.
Yet, when cross-fortune makes me move the brow,
Thine, without motion, better far doth show.
But by ill fortune oft though marred it be
It had good fortune to be made by thee;
For thou dost Fortune's furrows quite out-strike
And maks't it in all fortunes look alike.[84]

9 Science and Superstition

Rowse called the Renaissance "a betwixt and between world."[85] This was especially true of science during the Elizabethan Era. Although a handful of brilliant men made momentous strides, such as William Harvey's discovery of the circulation of blood, most people still believed in magic and witchcraft. Historian Lacey Baldwin Smith wrote:

> Sixteenth-century scientific truth was a strange composite of the old and new, chemistry and alchemy, astronomy and astrology, mathematics and numerology, medicine and magic, observation and sorcery. A bold mind might

lift a corner of the curtain of ignorance and glimpse the truth, but the man who dismissed astrology as nonsense might himself be a helpless devotee of occultism and cabala.[86]

Dr. John Dee was a perfect example. He was the outstanding mathematician of the first part of Elizabeth's reign, inventing new types of compasses and editing the English translation of the works of the Greek mathematician Euclid. He was devoted, however, to astrology (the prediction of events from the position of the stars, sun, moon, and planets) and was

Astrologers peer into the sky to predict future events. Astrologers were extremely popular with Elizabethans, who consulted them even in minor matters.

Queen Elizabeth's personal astrologer. In his later years, he became involved in crystal ball gazing and in alchemy (turning metals like lead or mercury into gold).

Astrology was so much a way of life that it became part of the language. We still speak of someone "born under a lucky star." Elizabeth once wrote Mary Queen of Scots that "I consider that by nature we are composed of earthly elements and governed by heavenly, and . . . I am not ignorant that our dispositions are caused in part by supernatural signs."[87]

Elizabethans used astrology both to predict the future and to try to control it. The queen had Dr. Dee cast the horoscopes (predictions based on the stars) of some of her various suitors. She asked him to consult his charts of the stars and planets before deciding on a day for her coronation, wanting to choose a day that would ensure a prosperous reign. When Elizabeth lay near death with smallpox in 1562, courtiers—wanting to be on the winning side—rushed to astrologers, asking them to cast the horoscopes of possible heirs to the throne. Astrologers were consulted even in small matters. Dr. Dee's clients sought his help in finding lost items—everything from a gold ring to a sack of flour.

Astrology and Agriculture

Astrology was considered vital to agriculture. Farmers planted crops according to the heavens. Thomas Tusser told them:

Sow peason and beans in the wane of
   the moon,
Who soweth them sooner, he soweth
   too soon;

That they with the planet may rest and
   arise
And flourish with bearing most plentiful wise.[88]

The annual almanac showing the phases of the moon and the relative positions of the moon and the sun was common by 1600. Even today, some farmers plant crops according to the phases of the moon, though there is no scientific evidence that such planting makes any difference in crops. Modern almanacs are much more helpful in giving predictions of weather patterns and soil conditions.

The comfortable, medieval view of the earth as the center of the universe—on which astrology was based—was shattered during the Elizabethan Era. A Polish astronomer, Nicolaus Copernicus, had published a book in 1543 arguing that the earth and the planets rotated around the sun. An Englishman, Thomas Digges, went beyond Copernicus and in 1576 theorized that stars really were other suns and that the universe had no boundaries.

Copernicus, Digges, and others who advocated the "heliocentric" (sun-centered) belief had a great impact on fellow scientists, but few outside the scientific community knew the traditional view was being challenged. That changed in 1572 when a new star appeared. It was what now is called a "supernova," and shone so brightly for fourteen months that it was visible even in the daytime. Its appearance "did more to shake Aristotelian [from the Greek philosopher Aristotle] physics and cosmology [astronomy] to ordinary minds than any amount of mathematical demonstration."[89] After all, the stars were supposed to have been fixed for all time by God at

Defending Copernicus

Mathematician Thomas Digges, in his 1576 paper entitled Prognostication Everlasting, *corrected the work of his father, Leonard, and defended the position of astronomer Nicolaus Copernicus, who had proposed that the earth and planets revolve around the sun. This passage is from* Elizabethan People: State and Society.

"Having of late, gentle Reader, corrected and reformed sundry faults that by negligence in printing have crept into my father's General Prognostication, among other things I found a description or model of the world and situation of spheres celestial and elementary according to the doctrine of Ptolomey [Ptolemy, an ancient Egyptian astronomer], whereunto all universities (led thereto chiefly by the authority of Aristotle [an ancient Greek philosopher]) since then have consented. But in our age one rare wit (seeing the continual errors that from time to time more and more have been discovered, besides the infinite absurdities in their theorickes, which they have been forced to admit that would not confess any mobility in the ball of the earth) hath by long study, painful practice, and rare invention delivered a new theorick or model of the world, shewing that the earth resteth not in the centre of the whole world, but only in the centre of this our mortal world or globe of elements, which environed and enclosed in the moon's orb, and together with the whole globe of mortality is carried yearly round the sun, which like a king in the midst of all reigneth and giveth the laws of motion to the rest, spherically dispersing his glorious beams of light through all this sacred celestial temple. . . . So many ways is the sense of mortal men abused, but reason and deep discourse of wit having opened these things to Copernicus . . . I thought it convenient together with the old theorick also to publish this, to the end such noble English minds . . . might not be altogether defrauded of so noble a part of philosophy."

Although his ideas would not be accepted during Elizabeth's reign, Nicolaus Copernicus was the first to argue that the earth revolved around the sun.

the Creation, according to the biblical Book of Genesis. It was not until the following century that the heliocentric view came to be generally accepted, but the supernova was the beginning of the end of astrology as a science.

Astrology and Medicine

The widespread belief in astrology extended to medicine. One of England's leading doctors, William Clowes, was a pioneer in the use of mercury to treat syphilis, a cure that, while effective, often poisoned the patient. Clowes believed, however, that signs of the zodiac governed various parts of the body. He would refuse to cut on an arm, for instance, if the sign at that particular time was the one supposedly governing the arm. He wrote, "I judge it very dangerous to touch any part of man's body with lancet or knife whenas the moon hath motion in that sign [of the zodiac] which governeth the part that should be striken."[90]

Indeed, medicine in Elizabethan England was largely medieval mumbo-jumbo. Edward Topsell wrote a popular book in which he claimed that the eyes of dragons "being kept till they be stale and afterwards beat into an oil with honey and made into an ointment keep anyone that useth it from the terror of night visions."[91] There were plenty of unscrupulous doctors who claimed to have such ingredients and who sold their potions to trusting patients.

Outlandish remedies were common. Powdered armadillo bone was supposed to cure deafness. A dead mouse, cut in half and placed on a wart, was supposed to remove it. Scrofula, a knotty tumor just under the skin,

The signs of the Zodiac ruled the philosophy of leading physician William Clowes, who refused to operate on patients when zodiac signs seemed unfavorable.

was called the "King's Evil," because it supposedly could be cured by a touch of a ruler's hand. Clowes said that such tumors could not be cured by surgery but rather by "a divine and holy curation, which is most admirable to the world, that I have seen and known performed and done by the sacred hands of the Queen's most royal Majesty."[92] The practice continued in England until the 1700s.

Most modern-day medicines were completely unknown. Although a few diseases were treated with chemicals such as mercury, zinc, and arsenic, these often did more harm than good. Natural treatments, such as herbs, were more popular, and sometimes worked, although doctors

Medical Tips for Children

In his autobiography, Lord Herbert of Cherbury gave these hints for treating sick children. It shows Elizabethan medicine's reliance on herbs. The passage is found in Elizabethan People: State and Society.

"And first, I find, that in the infants those diseases are to be remedied which may be hereditary unto them on either side; so that, if they be subject to the [gall]stone or gravel, I do conceive it will be good for the nurse [breast-feeding the baby] sometimes to drink posset drinks, in which are boiled such things as are good to expel gravel and stone; the child also himself when he comes to some age may use the same posset drinks of herbs, as milium solis, saxifragia, etc., good for the stone many are reckoned by the physicians, of which also myself could bring a large catalogue, but rather leave it to those who are expert in that art. The same course is to be taken for the gout; for which purpose I do much commend the bathing of children's legs and feet in the water wherein smiths quench their iron, as also water wherein alum hath been infused, or boiled, as also the decoction of juniper berries, bay berries, chamædrys chemæpitys, which baths also are good for those that are hereditarily subject to the palsy, for these things do much strengthen the sinews; as also olium castorii, and sucini, which are not be used without advice. They that are also subject to the spleen from their ancestors, ought to use those herbs that are splenetics: and those that are troubled with the falling sickness, with cephaniques. . . . Briefly, what disease soever it be that is derived from ancestors of either side, it will be necessary first to give such medicines to the nurse as may make her milk effectual for those purposes; as also afterwards to give unto the child itself such specific remedies as his age and constitution will bear."

seldom knew why. Most Elizabethan botanists (scientists who study plants) were also doctors. One, Sir John Salusbury, prescribed this remedy for a backache:

Good sir if you lack the strengthe in your
    back
and would have a Remediado
Take Eryngo [ginger] rootes and Mary
    bone tartes
    Redd wine and rich Potato
An oyster pie and a Lobsters thigh
    hard eggs well dressed in Marrow
This will ease your backes disease

and make you a good Cocksparrowe.
An Apricock or an Artichoke
  Anchovies oyle and Pepper
These to use doe not refuse
  twill make your back the better.[93]

Laying the Blame

Little could be done to cure diseases because no one really knew what caused
them. Some people blamed the stars when
they became ill. Some thought gluttony or
drunkenness was the cause. Some blamed
England's cold, damp climate. During
widespread outbreaks of disease, such as
the plague, Jews were accused of poison-
ing wells. It was not until the invention of
the microscope in the next century that
scientists could see what caused disease
and how it was spread.

Doctors were helpless in the face of
epidemics. The plague, or Black Death,
had first broken out in Europe in the mid-
1300s and reappeared frequently. About
twenty thousand Londoners were killed in
1563 and 30,500 in 1603. Doctors and city
officials knew the plague was highly conta-
gious, but had no idea how it was spread.
They knew the bodies of the dead should
be avoided, that their houses should be
shut up, and that garbage should be
burned. Their orders were mostly ignored. Elizabethan government was "in-
sufficiently organised to carry out with
success an elaborate set of unpopular orders . . . the authorities were forced to sit
with folded hands until the plague had
spent itself."[94]

Instead, the people relied on folk wisdom. They crowded around burial pits at
funerals because they believed no one

*Elizabethans were helpless in the face of the Black
Death, which decimated the population. Many
unscientific theories were offered for the plague's
causes.*

could be infected while attending a religious service. Some treated the plague by
holding plucked chickens against the
buboes (sores) to draw out the poison.

Surgery was still highly primitive. The
Royal College of Surgeons had been
formed in 1540 by merging the surgeons'
and barbers' guilds, and many surgeons
were still also barbers. Surgeons, however,
were not considered doctors. In fact, they
were prohibited from practicing medicine
by the rival Royal College of Physicians,
which wanted to keep a monopoly on the
profession. Still, some advances were

made. Frenchman Ambrose Paré developed a method of ligating (sewing shut) stumps after amputation of arms or legs instead of cauterizing (sealing with boiling pitch or a red-hot iron). Paré was wise enough, however, to know the extent of his own ignorance and not to take too much credit. "I treated him," he said, "and God cured him."[95]

Mental Illness

The Elizabethans were the first to begin to understand the causes of mental illnesses. Timothy Bright, in his *Treatise of Melancholy* in 1586, suggested that some mental illnesses were caused by "a certain fearful disposition of the mind," and prescribed such things as cheerful music, rest, and a

A popular treatment for just about any ailment was bloodletting. Unfortunately, on an already ill and weak patient, bloodletting often caused death rather than cure.

light diet.[96] Previously, doctors thought mental illness was caused by "evil humours" (bodily fluids) that could be reduced by bloodletting. This treatment consisted of taking blood from a patient by cutting a vein or attaching a blood-sucking leech.

Often, people with mental illnesses were thought to be possessed by devils or, worse, were thought to be the victims of witchcraft. Even university scholars and high church officials believed in witches. Many rural villages had "cunning" women, folk healers who brewed their own medicines, which often proved more effective than those of doctors.

The persecution of witches was never as widespread in England as in the rest of Europe. The English were as superstitious as anyone, but the kind of blind obsession that saw thousands burned at the stake in Germany was foreign to the English character. Thirty persons were hanged for witchcraft in the first twenty years of Elizabeth's reign, but that was a small number compared with the number of those executed for other crimes—forty in 1598 alone for the single county of Somerset.

New World Exploration

Many of the great scientific accomplishments of the Elizabethan Age resulted from the exploration of the New World. In 1585, when Sir Walter Raleigh sent his first expedition to colonize North America, he included Thomas Hariot, the first great English anthropologist (one who studies human society). Raleigh wanted Hariot to study not only the plants and an-

Witches are executed in sixteenth-century England. The witch craze in England never gained the level of hysteria that it did in the rest of Europe.

imals but also the Native Americans of what would become Virginia. Hariot's book, *Briefe and True Report of the New Found Land of Virginia,* was the recognized authority for the next century on life in North America. He described native animals and plants, including tobacco, which would soon be popular in England. He learned the language of the natives and wrote about their customs.

Hariot also was a skilled physicist and astronomer and used his knowledge to give Raleigh improved navigational charts and instruments. He invented a new instrument for observing the sun and calculating a ship's position on the sea. He was the first to compile a table that showed how to find due east or due west by observing where the sun rose or set.

Dr. William Gilbert was Europe's foremost expert on magnetism. His book *De Magnete,* published in 1600, described for the first time the earth's magnetic field, showing why a compass needle pointed north. He showed how rubbing certain objects, such as amber, made them attract light objects. He called such objects "electriks" and speculated on the force they generated, thus paving the way for the science of electronics. His discoveries led to vast improvements in compasses and other navigational instruments. His work also was a major influence on Sir Isaac Newton, who in another century would propose the law of gravity.

Francis Bacon

Perhaps the greatest scientific achievement of the Elizabethan Age, however, was not a single discovery. The man who made it, Francis Bacon, was known more as a philosopher and a politician than as a scientist. The accepted method of scientific investigation had been to form a theory and then try to prove it. Bacon said,

The Medical Profession

In his Advancement of Learning *written in 1605, Francis Bacon discusses what he believes to be the poor state of the medical profession. It is found in* Elizabethan People: State and Society.

"Nay, we see the weakness and credulity of men is such, as they will often prefer a mountebank or witch before a learned physician. . . . And what followeth? Even this, that physicians say to themselves, as Solomon expresseth it upon a higher occasion: 'If it befal me as befalleth to the fools, why should I labour to be more wise?' And therefore I cannot much blame physicians that they use commonly to intend some other art or practice, which they fancy, more than their profession. For you shall have them antiquaries, poets, humanists, statesmen, merchants, divines, and in every of these better seen than in their profession; and no doubt upon this ground, that they find that mediocrity and excellency in their art maketh no difference in profit or reputation toward their fortunes. . . . Medicine is a science which hath been (as we have said) more professed than laboured, and yet more laboured than advanced; the labour having been, in my judgment, rather in circle than in progression. For I find much iteration, but small addition."

Sir Francis Bacon introduced the method of scientific investigation to medicine. More of a philosopher than a scientist, Bacon argued that all scientific conclusions should be based on observable phenomenon and fact.

instead, that knowledge can come only from experimentation and observation of facts. He said that instead of *deduction*—starting with a general assumption and working down to specifics—science should be *inductive*—arriving at a general conclusion based on observations.

Bacon was one of the first persons in history to combine science with philosophy. He argued that humanity—not nature—is the primary shaper of events and that it is up to people, through observation and experiments, to use nature to make life on earth better. He recog-

Dr. William Gilbert presents his experiments on electricity to the queen and her court. Gilbert's discoveries led to the science of magnetism and electronics.

nized that science is not a set of disconnected discoveries, but that each sets the stage for another. He wrote that the important part of history is not wars or conquests, but the development of ideas and thought.

Bacon's view of inductive, or experimental, science quickly became popular. It did not eventually become the prevailing procedure; deductive science remains the preferred method of discovery. His concept, however, greatly influenced the ex-perimental scientists of the next century, including the astronomer Galileo.

Bacon's writing also led a group of scientists to begin holding meetings to discuss their experiments. This group eventually became the world's most famous scientific organization, the Royal Society. When the history of the society was written, it said that Bacon was "the one great man, who had the true imagination of the whole extent of this enterprise, as it is now set on foot."[97]

10 Toward the New World

When England finally joined her European neighbors in the exploration of the New World, more than half a century had passed since Christopher Columbus's 1492 voyage. The English made up for their late start with the boldness that marked the age. By the end of Elizabeth's reign, England was the world's leading sea power, was firmly established in North America, and had laid the foundations of the British Empire.

England's success was attributable to the intense interest of the country's leaders—including Elizabeth—in the profits to be made by the incredible bravery and

spirit of its sailors. "What shall we be?" Sir Walter Raleigh asked, "travelers or tinkers; conquerors or novices?"[98] Elizabeth's sailors endured terrible hardships and dangers. When they ran short of food on voyages (which was often), they ate everything except one another—including penguins on the southern tip of South America and polar bears in the Arctic. Their exploits began the legend of English sea power, which was to reach a peak with the defeat of the great Spanish fleet, the Armada, in 1588.

Elizabeth's grandfather, Henry VII, made only a small attempt to explore

The English were latecomers to exploration. Only one major voyage was attempted by Henry VII, who sent John Cabot on a voyage to find the Northwest Passage in 1497.

John Hawkins attempts to fend off an attack by Spanish ships at St. Juan de Ulloa.

the Americas. In 1497, he sent an English sea captain, John Cabot, on a voyage to what is now Greenland, Nova Scotia, and Newfoundland. Cabot was looking both for riches and for the Northwest Passage, a way around America into the Pacific Ocean. He found neither, and Henry soon lost interest.

While Elizabeth's father, Henry VIII, was busy squandering money in France and feuding with the pope about his divorce, Spain conquered Mexico and Peru and Portugal founded colonies in India and the Philippines. The real start of English exploration and trade came with the reign of Elizabeth's brother, Edward VI. Hugh Willoughby and Richard Chancellor led an expedition in 1553 that went around Scandinavia to the north to try to find a Northeast Passage to Asia. The expedition failed to find any passage, but it opened trade between England and Russia.

The other area of English activity was West Africa, which supposedly was the ex-clusive territory of Portugal. In 1493, Pope Alexander VI had divided the unknown lands of Africa and the Americas between Spain and Portugal. This, however, did not stop the sailors of Protestant England. Thomas Windham began trading on the Barbary Coast and Gold Coast in the early 1550s. The Portuguese "were much offended with this our new trade into Barbary . . . and gave out that if they took us in those parts, they would use us as their mortal enemies."[99]

Hawkins's Voyages

The first great voyages under Elizabeth were those of John Hawkins. Hawkins, whose father had also been a sea captain, knew that the Spanish in the New World needed labor for their plantations. He sailed to Guinea in 1562, bought or captured about three hundred Africans, and sailed to the West

Indies where he sold them as slaves. The trip was so profitable that Elizabeth herself invested in his next one, which was just as much a moneymaker.

By the time Hawkins made his third voyage, however, King Philip of Spain no longer wanted Englishmen in his domains. In 1568, Hawkins's ships were at San Juan de Ulloa when a large Spanish fleet appeared at the mouth of the Mexican harbor. Rather than exchange gunfire with Hawkins, the Spanish commander signaled that the English would be allowed to leave. Then, when the Spaniards were close enough, they rushed and boarded the English ships. Only two ships escaped—the *Minion*, with Hawkins in command, and the *Judith*, commanded by one of Hawkins's best young captains, Francis Drake.

San Juan de Ulloa ended the friendship that had existed between England and Spain since the previous century. Not only did England think its ships had been taken by treachery, but many of the captured sailors were harshly treated. Some were burned at the stake for their Protestant beliefs. A. L. Rowse wrote, "One must not . . . underestimate the force of the hatred for Spain all this piled up among the Protestants of Europe."[100]

Elizabeth wanted revenge and she wanted more profits from America, but she did not want war with Spain. She promised Philip that English adventures in America would stop, but she secretly encouraged them. The result was a decade of undeclared war on Spain by English privateers—mainly by Drake.

Drake was one of the outstanding figures, not only of the Elizabethan Age, but in all English history. He was the most famous of Elizabeth's subjects, loved by the English for his boldness and feared by the Spanish, who called him "El Draque" (the Dragon). Englishmen loved to tell about him raiding the Spanish harbor of Cadiz in 1587 and "singeing the King of Spain's beard."[101] The story goes that Drake was bowling when informed that the Spanish Armada had been sighted off Plymouth in England. "We have time to finish the game and beat the Spaniards, too," he is

Sir Francis Drake climbs a tree to gain his first view of the Pacific Ocean in 1572. Drake's prayers that he might someday sail the Pacific would be answered by Elizabeth.

Francis Drake takes on a Spanish galleon in 1588. Drake's mission was plunder rather than exploration. Little more than a pirate, Drake robbed Spain of her riches by harassing her ships on the high seas.

supposed to have said.[102] It was Drake who gave the English their reputation as being unconquerable at sea.

Drake's Adventures

Drake's first voyage, in 1571, was mainly to look over Spanish territory in the Caribbean to find the likeliest targets. On the second, in 1572–73, he captured the town of Nombre de Dios in Panama and made off with £40,000 in gold and silver from Spanish mines in Peru. When he arrived back in Plymouth on a Sunday morning, word spread throughout the city, even into St. Andrew's Church. The people were so filled "with desire and delight to see him that very few or none remained with the preacher."[103]

While in Panama, Drake had climbed a high tree from which he could see the Pacific Ocean and prayed that he might someday sail those waters. Elizabeth had

refused others permission to raid Spanish possessions on America's western coast, but in 1577 she approved Drake's plan to conduct such a raid, saying, "Drake! So it is that I would gladly be revenged on the King of Spain for divers injuries that I have received."[104]

Drake's Pacific voyage had plenty of backers, including Elizabeth, Leicester, Hawkins, and Walsingham. When rumors of the expedition reached Spain and Philip complained, Elizabeth wrote him personally, saying, "We beg very affectionately that all suspicions may be banished from between us, if any such have been raised by the acts of wicked men with the object of destroying the close friendship which we enjoyed in our earlier years."[105]

The voyage, begun in 1577, had all the elements of an adventure yarn—violent storms at sea, shortages of food, even an unsuccessful mutiny. Of his three ships, only Drake's flagship, the *Pelican*, made it through the Strait of Magellan on the tip of South America. Drake renamed his ship the *Golden*

Hind (dog), the symbol of one of his chief sponsors, Lord Hatton, and began attacking the unsuspecting and undefended Spanish settlements along the coasts of Chile and Peru and capturing Spanish ships.

Drake's objective was plunder, not punishment. He did not kill Spaniards unless attacked, and he treated prisoners graciously. One Spanish captain gave this account:

> When our ship was sacked, no [English] man dared take anything without his orders: he shows them great favour, but punishes the least fault. . . . Each one takes particular pains to keep his arquebus [a type of gun] clean. He also carried painters who paint for him pictures of the coast in exact colours.

He carried trained carpenters and artisans, so as to be able to careen the ship at any time. . . . He is served on silver dishes with gold borders and gilded garlands. . . . He dines and sups to the music of viols.[106]

The Queue Is Pleased

Drake continued up the coast, then crossed the Pacific, went around India and Africa and back to England. He arrived in Plymouth after a voyage of thirty-four months. His first question on entering the harbor was whether Elizabeth was alive and well. Indeed she was! And she was

Elizabeth knights Francis Drake aboard his ship the Golden Hind. *Drake was a favorite of the queen because she personally benefitted from his piratical exploits.*

The New World Learns About Elizabeth

Elizabeth was praised far and wide, even in the New World, as this passage from The Discovery of Guiana *by Sir Walter Raleigh shows. It is found in* The Horizon Book of the Elizabethan World.

"We then hastened away toward our purposed discovery, and first I called all the captains [native chiefs] of the islands together that were enemies to the Spaniards, for there were some which Berrio [a Spanish official] had brought out of other countries and planted there to eat out and waste those that were natural of the place, and by my Indian interpreter, which I carried out of England, I made them understand that I was the servant of a queen, who was the great cacique [chief] of the north, and a virgin and had more caciques under her than there were trees in that island: that she was an enemy to the Castelani [Spaniards] to respect of their tyranny and oppression, and that she delivered all such nations about her as were by them oppressed, and having freed all the coast of the northern world from their servitude had sent me to free them also, and with all to defend the country of Guiana from their invasion and conquest. I showed them Her Majesty's picture, which they so admired and honored, as it had been easy to have brought them idolatrous thereof."

pleased with Drake for his exploits and even more pleased with the treasure he brought her. She even went to visit him on the *Golden Hind.* When he knelt before her, she joked that she had a sword ready to cut off his head. Instead, she made him a knight. When the Spanish ambassador demanded that Drake be brought to trial for piracy and the treasure returned, Elizabeth claimed not to know what he was talking about.

Drake's voyage around the world and his success against the supposedly all-powerful Spanish raised the world's opinion of England. More important, it raised England's opinion of itself. Richard Hakluyt, whose account of Elizabethan explorations was published in 1589, boasted:

What ever ships did heretofore . . . pass and repass the unpassable (in former opinion) strait of Magellan, range along the coast of Chile, Peru and all the backside of nova Hispania, further than any Christian ever passed, traverse the mighty breadth of the South Sea . . . and traffic with the princes of the Moluccas . . . and last of all return home most richly laden with the commodities of China, as the

Drake in Chile

The western coast of South America was largely undefended when Sir Francis Drake raided it on his voyage in 1577–79. This account from Richard Hakluyt's Voyages and Documents *is found in* The Horizon Book of the Elizabethan World.

"And when they had come thither [the city of Santiago], they found the same ship and in her three Negroes and eight Spaniards; they of the ship, thinking Drake's to have been Spaniards, welcomed them with a drum and made ready a great barrel of wine of Chile to have made them drink; but when Drake's men were entered, one of them, whose name was Tom Moone, struck the Spanish pilot with his fist on the face, saying 'Abassho pirra,' which is to say in English, 'Go down, dog,' and then the poor Spaniards being sore afraid went down into the hold of the ship, all saving one of them, who, leaping out at the stern of the ship swam on shore and gave warning to them of the town of their coming. When Drake had taken this ship and stowed the men under hatches, he took her boat and his own boat and manned them both with his men, and went to set upon the town of Santiago, having not passed eight or nine small houses, and coming on shore, he found all the people fled, and rifled their houses, and broke open a warehouse, wherein he found certain wine of Chile, which he brought with him into his ship; also he found there a chapel, which he rifled and took from thence a chalice of silver and two cruets of silver . . . and the altar cloth, all which he took away with him and brought them on board, and gave the spoil of that chapel to Mr. Fletcher, his preacher, at his coming on board; and then he set all of the men of the Spanish ship on shore, saving one John Grego, a Greek born, whom he took with him to be his pilot to bring him into the harbor of Lima. This Spanish ship Drake took along with him and rifled her, and found in her great store of wine of Chile, and about four hundred pounds weight of gold of Baldivia, which is a city and lies about four leagues from Santiago up into the land, from whence cometh the best gold of all Peru."

Mary Queen of Scots is led to her execution. Mary's execution led to increased conflict between Catholic Spain and mostly Protestant England.

subjects of this now flourishing monarchy have done?[107]

Ironically, much of Drake's Spanish treasure went to help the Dutch, who were rebelling against their Spanish overlords. His adventures made war between England and Spain almost inevitable.

The other factor that led to open warfare between England and Spain was the execution of Mary Queen of Scots in 1587. Throughout her long confinement, Mary had delighted in scheming against Elizabeth, spinning plots and sending out secret messages. Her brother-in-law, King Charles IX of France, said, "Ah! The poor fool will never cease until she loses her

head."[108] That is exactly what happened.

Elizabeth's councillors had long pleaded with her to have Mary executed. Elizabeth would not be sorry to see Mary die, but she refused to give the order. Finally, she was persuaded to sign Mary's death warrant. Even then, she refused to actually order the sentence carried out. She told a secretary, William Davidson, only to deliver it to the Lord Chancellor, not to take the final step of sending it to Fotheringhay Castle, where Mary was being kept. Burghley and Elizabeth's other advisers, who desired Mary's death, immediately sent the warrant on its way before the queen could change her mind, and Mary was beheaded.

The Spanish Armada

Mary's death opened the way for an invasion of England by Spain. Philip II, even after Elizabeth rejected his offer of marriage, long supported her right to rule, even though he was a Catholic and she a Protestant. He knew that if she were succeeded by Mary Queen of Scots, England would become an ally of France. Now, Mary was dead, and a successful invasion would make Philip ruler of England instead of Mary.

Spain and England had long been on a collision course. It was difficult for Philip, as the most powerful, most religious Catholic king in Europe, to stand by while a Protestant kingdom flourished. Moreover, England was flourishing at Spain's expense, thanks mainly to Drake's voyages.

At last, Philip had enough. He began to build a mighty fleet of ships, the Armada, designed to sail from Spain, pick up the Duke of Parma's Spanish army in the

Netherlands, and invade England. The Armada, more than 130 ships strong, sailed in May 1588.

Elizabeth had not wanted war. To her, war was a waste of money. Yet, when war came, she went in person to rally her soldiers, who would have to defend the country should her navy fail to stop the Armada. Addressing the troops, she said:

> I am come amongst you as you see, at this time, not for my recreation and disport, but being resolved, in the midst and heat of the battle, to live or die amongst you all, and to lay down for my God and for my kingdome and for my people, my honor and my blood, even in the dust. I know I have the body of a weak and feeble woman, but I have the heart and stomach of a king, and of a king of England too and think foul scorn that Parma or Spain, or any prince of Europe should dare to invade the borders of my realm.[109]

The soldiers, as it happened, were not needed. The English navy, commanded by Charles Howard, along with Sir Francis Drake and John Hawkins, defeated the Spaniards, not in a great battle, but in a series of skirmishes in the English Channel. The Armada was forced to return home by sailing all the way around Scotland and Ireland and lost more than half its ships.

Consequences of Battle

The defeat of the Spanish Armada was a major turning point in world history. Spain was the strongest nation in Europe, and the Armada had been considered the finest, most powerful fleet ever assembled. Its defeat marked the beginning of Spain's long decline as a world power. She still was powerful, but the peak of Spanish might had passed.

The defeat of the Armada also was a blow to the Roman Catholic church. First, it ensured that England would remain Protestant. There would be no more serious attempts to return the English church to the pope's rule. Second, it weakened Spain to the point where the Netherlands were able to shake off Spanish domination,

The Spanish Armada sails up the English Channel to its defeat. By defeating Spain, England inherited the title of the world's most powerful seagoing nation.

thus enabling the Protestant Dutch to stay independent of the Catholic church.

For England, however, the victory was the start of a rise to prominence. The island nation, which had been lightly regarded by the rest of Europe, was now considered a power to be reckoned with. Also, with the threat of invasion removed, England could begin her own program of colonization in the Americas and elsewhere—a program that would lead eventually to the establishment of the British Empire.

Just as important, the victory created a spirit of national pride and confidence among the English. With this spirit came a burst of creativity in science, literature, and drama. While the Elizabethan Age began with the young queen's coronation, most of the greatest achievements—Shakespeare's

---

A Lion at Sea

English explorers encountered all sorts of unfamiliar animals. This "lion" described by Edward Hare, who sailed with Sir Humphrey Gilbert to Newfoundland, was probably a walrus. The description is found in The Horizon Book of the Elizabethan World.

"So upon Saturday in the afternoon of the thirty-first of August, we changed our course and returned back for England, at which very instant, even in winding about, there passed along between us and toward the land which we now forsook a very lion to our seeming, in shape, hair, and color, not swimming after the manner of a beast by moving of his feet, but rather sliding upon the water with his whole body (excepting the legs) in sight, neither yet diving under and again rising above the water, as the manner is of whales, dolphines, tunnies [tuna], porpoises, and all other fish, but confidently showing himself above water without hiding; notwithstanding, we presented ourselves in open view and gesture to amaze him, as all creatures will be commonly at a sudden gaze and sight of men. Thus he passed along turning his head to and fro, yawning and gaping wide, with ugly demonstration of long teeth and glaring eyes, and to bid us a farewell . . . he sent forth a horrible voice, roaring or bellowing as doth a lion, which spectacle we all beheld so far as we were able to discern the same, as men prone to wonder at every strange thing, as this doubtless was, to see a lion in the ocean sea, or fish in shape of a lion."

plays, the colonization of North America—were packed into the two decades following the defeat of the Armada.

The Virginia Colony

In 1584, Raleigh received a charter from Elizabeth empowering him "to discover barbarous countries, not actually possessed of any Christian prince and inhabited by Christian people, to occupy and enjoy the same for ever."[110] The next year, an expedition commanded by Raleigh's cousin, Sir Richard Grenville, established a colony of one hundred men on Roanoke Island, off the coast of what Raleigh named Virginia, in honor of Elizabeth, the "Virgin Queen."

The first Roanoke colony lasted only a year because of a lack of supplies. Most of the colonists returned to England, leaving behind only fifteen men. Raleigh reestablished the colony in 1587, this time bringing seventeen women along with one hundred men. The inclusion of women showed that England's goal was a permanent settlement, an extension of England itself, rather than a trading post.

Because of the war with Spain, supply ships were not sent to Roanoke until 1590. The colonists had disappeared, probably massacred by Indians. Ever since, Roanoke has been known as the "Lost Colony." The English were so disappointed that no new settlement was attempted until after Elizabeth's death, when permanent colonies were founded at Jamestown in Virginia (1607) and in Guiana in South America (1609).

The start of English colonization was the beginning of the British Empire. The colonies themselves were established un-

Sir Walter Raleigh arrives at Roanoke Island to form an English colony in the New World. The colony at Roanoke mysteriously disappeared, although most believe the settlers were massacred by Native Americans.

der Elizabeth's successors, but they had been made possible only by the grand spirit of exploration and adventure that was part of the Elizabethan Era. England's colonies would be far different from those of other European countries. As Lacey Baldwin Smith wrote:

> Of the imperial powers, only England succeeded in transplanting its people and establishing small, tough, and vital replicas of itself on the inhospitable shores and in the endless forests of an uncharted land. . . . Only England sent out viable offshoots with men to toil, women to be fruitful, children to endure the future, and laws by which to live.[111]

The Elizabethan Heritage

With the defeat of the Armada, Elizabeth was almost sixty years old and beginning to outlive some of the people closest to her. Leicester died shortly after the victory. Burghley died in 1598, and the queen grew more and more lonely.

Elizabeth gradually became less active and more temperamental, often lashing out at those around her. Still, she could be regal. Addressing Parliament for the last time in November 1601, she said:

> Though God hath raised me high, yet this I count the glory of my crown, that I have reigned with your loves. . . .

It is not my desire to live or reign longer than my life and reign shall be for your good. And though you have had, and may have, many mightier and wiser princes sitting in this seat, yet you never had, nor shall have, any that will love you better.[112]

Elizabeth died on March 24, 1603. She was sixty-nine years old, an age no English monarch before her had reached. Shortly after her eyes closed for the last time, a rider sped north to tell the news to England's new king, James, son of Elizabeth's old rival, Mary Queen of Scots.

An elaborate funeral was held for Elizabeth, who died in 1603 at the age of sixty-nine. By the end of her reign, Elizabeth had proven her abilities as a great monarch.

The Elizabethan Age lingered for years after the death of Elizabeth. Many of Shakespeare's best plays were written after 1603. Jamestown, Virginia, was settled in 1607. Dr. William Harvey discovered the circulation of blood in 1617. Indeed, the spirit of innovation, discovery, and accomplishment that distinguished the age continued until the Civil War in 1642 and the triumph of the Puritan Parliament.

Elizabeth had given much more than her name to her reign. For all her faults—vanity, temper, and deceit—she was exactly what England needed in 1558, someone to steer the country through the treacherous and dangerous decades to a time of prosperity never before known. St. Clair Byrne wrote that "she created in a whole people a passionate loyalty, half personal, half national, wholly English, which was the one thing necessary if the promise of Tudor England was to be fulfilled."[113] The English recognized their debt to their queen. An Act of Parliament in 1601 said that "no age either hath or can produce the like precedent of so much happiness under any prince's reign."[114] Nothing, however, expressed what the English felt for Elizabeth more than the scribblings of a schoolboy, John Slye, who wrote in the margin of a book in 1589:

The rose is redd, the leves are grene.
God save Elizabeth, our noble Quene.[115]

A Living Legacy

In many ways, the Elizabethan Era never ended. Its achievements have echoed through the centuries. Much of the world

Although the Elizabethan Era today is remembered for its contribution to the arts, in her time, Elizabeth's major accomplishment was to end the bloody internal religious conflicts that had plagued England for years.

owes such basic elements as language, law, and religion to the Elizabethans. As Rowse wrote, "The Elizabethan Age is not something dead and apart from us: it is alive and all round us and within us . . . part of our living experience, entering into our conscious tradition and into the secret channels of heart and blood."[116]

One of the greatest contributions of Elizabethan England is the English language itself. A prominent linguist wrote that "no other half century has done so much for the permanent enrichment of the language as that which is covered by Shakespeare's lifetime."[117] The credit for this goes to the Elizabethan writers. Of these, Shakespeare towers above all the rest. It is doubtful that any writer in history better captured the soul of his language and of his people. Not only the language, but also the feeling of Elizabethan England comes to us through his plays and poetry. As one scholar said, "It is astonishing how little out of touch with Shakespeare and his age we are. . . . We have changed in the things we *do;* but how little yet have those things changed us in what we *are.*"[118]

Of all the accomplishments of the Elizabethan Age, one is due mostly to the queen personally—the Church of England. She rejected the Catholic church, but would not allow the Puritans and other reformers to go too far. She "gave the English Church [a] chance to take root, to grow into the minds and hearts of later generations."[119] Every bride or groom who has repeated the words "for better for worse, for richer for poorer, in sickness and health, to love and to cherish, till death us do part" can thank Elizabeth, who ensured the survival of the Church of England prayer book containing the famous vow.

The entire Elizabethan experience—religion, language, drama—would not have spread so far and so fast had it not been for the great burst of exploration and colonization. Rowse wrote, "The English entered late, but in the end most effectively of all—and that was the work of the Elizabethans. . . . They foreshadowed the ways their people were to take in the centuries to come."[120] England's concept of law and its representative form of government, as well as its language and religion, were carried everywhere from America to India.

The Elizabethan Era has inspired not only the English, but people throughout the world—Americans, Indians, Africans, Canadians, Jamaicans, Egyptians—people everywhere who, at one time or another, were part of the British Empire. Many British colonies, such as the United States, went their own ways. Yet they owe much of their culture to Elizabeth's England. It was "one of those rare periods when the past and the future are both coloured by imagination, and both shed a glory on the present."[121]

Notes

Introduction: The English Renaissance

1. Quoted in Carolly Erickson, *The First Elizabeth*. New York: Summit Books, 1983.
2. Quoted in Erickson, *The First Elizabeth*.
3. A. L. Rowse, *The Elizabethan Renaissance: The Life of the Society*. New York: Charles Scribner's Sons, 1971.
4. A. H. Dodd, *Elizabethan England*. New York: G. P. Putnam's Sons, 1973.

Chapter 1: Gloriana and Her Court

5. Quoted in Lacey Baldwin Smith, *The Horizon Book of the Elizabethan World*. New York: American Heritage, 1967.
6. Quoted in Christopher Morris, *The Tudors*. Glasgow, Scotland: Fontana Collins, 1966.
7. Quoted in Milton Waldman, *Rod of Iron*. Boston: Houghton Mifflin, 1941.
8. Quoted in Smith, *The Horizon Book of the Elizabethan World*.
9. Quoted in Elizabeth Jenkins, *Elizabeth the Great*. New York: Capricorn Books, 1967.
10. Quoted in Smith, *The Horizon Book of the Elizabethan World*.
11. Quoted in Jenkins, *Elizabeth the Great*.
12. Quoted in Dodd, *Elizabethan England*.
13. Quoted in Rowse, *The Elizabethan Renaissance: The Life of the Society*.
14. Quoted in Morris, *The Tudors*.
15. Quoted in Morris, *The Tudors*.
16. Quoted in Morris, *The Tudors*.
17. Quoted in Erickson, *The First Elizabeth*.
18. Quoted in Erickson, *The First Elizabeth*.
19. Quoted in Rowse, *The Elizabethan Renaissance: The Life of the Society*.
20. Rowse, *The Elizabethan Renaissance: The Life of the Society*.

Chapter 2: London and the Towns

21. Quoted in A. L. Rowse, *The England of Elizabeth*. New York: Collier Books, 1950.
22. A. L. Rowse, *The England of Elizabeth*.
23. Quoted in M. St. Clair Byrne, *Elizabethan Life in Town and Country*. London: Methuen, 1961.
24. Quoted in Byrne, *Elizabethan Life in Town and Country*.
25. Quoted in Rowse, *The Elizabethan Renaissance: The Life of the Society*.
26. Quoted in Byrne, *Elizabethan Life in Town and Country*.
27. Quoted in Robert Gray, *A History of London*. New York: Taplinger, 1978.
28. Quoted in Byrne, *Elizabethan Life in Town and Country*.
29. Quoted in Byrne, *Elizabethan Life in Town and Country*.
30. Quoted in Byrne, *Elizabethan Life in Town and Country*.
31. Quoted in Dodd, *Elizabethan England*.
32. Rowse, *The England of Elizabeth*.

Chapter 3: Life in the Countryside

33. Quoted in Byrne, *Elizabethan Life in Town and Country*.
34. Quoted in Rowse, *The England of Elizabeth*.
35. Quoted in Rowse, *The England of Elizabeth*.
36. Quoted in Byrne, *Elizabethan Life in Town and Country*.
37. Quoted in Byrne, *Elizabethan Life in Town and Country*.
38. Quoted in Byrne, *Elizabethan Life in Town and Country*.

39. Quoted in Byrne, *Elizabethan Life in Town and Country*.

40. Quoted in Rowse, *The England of Elizabeth*.

41. Quoted in Byrne, *Elizabethan Life in Town and Country*.

Chapter 4: Social Classes and Government

42. Quoted in Rowse, *The England of Elizabeth*.

43. Dodd, *Elizabethan England*.

44. Rowse, *The England of Elizabeth*.

45. Quoted in Rowse, *The England of Elizabeth*.

46. Quoted in Rowse, *The England of Elizabeth*.

47. Quoted in Rowse, *The England of Elizabeth*.

48. Quoted in Byrne, *Elizabethan Life in Town and Country*.

49. Quoted in Rowse, *The England of Elizabeth*.

50. Quoted in Byrne, *Elizabethan Life in Town and Country*.

51. Quoted in Rowse, *The England of Elizabeth*.

52. Rowse, *The England of Elizabeth*.

53. Quoted in Rowse, *The England of Elizabeth*.

54. Quoted in Rowse, *The England of Elizabeth*.

55. Rowse, *The England of Elizabeth*.

56. Rowse, *The England of Elizabeth*.

Chapter 5: Religion and the Church

57. Quoted in Rowse, *The England of Elizabeth*.

58. Quoted in Rowse, *The England of Elizabeth*.

59. Quoted in Rowse, *The England of Elizabeth*.

60. Rowse, *The England of Elizabeth*.

61. Quoted in Smith, *The Horizon Book of the Elizabethan World*.

Chapter 6: The Nation at Play

62. Quoted in Rowse, *The Elizabethan Renaissance: The Life of the Society*.

63. Quoted in Byrne, *Elizabethan Life in Town and Country*.

64. Quoted in Rowse, *The Elizabethan Renaissance: The Life of the Society*.

65. Quoted in Rowse, *The Elizabethan Renaissance: The Life of the Society*.

66. Byrne, *Elizabethan Life in Town and Country*.

67. Quoted in Byrne, *Elizabethan Life in Town and Country*.

68. Quoted in Rowse, *The Elizabethan Renaissance: The Life of the Society*.

69. Quoted in Rowse, *The Elizabethan Renaissance: The Life of the Society*.

70. Quoted in Erickson, *The First Elizabeth*.

71. Quoted in Byrne, *Elizabethan Life in Town and Country*.

72. Quoted in Byrne, *Elizabethan Life in Town and Country*.

Chapter 7: Elizabethan Drama

73. G. B. Harrison, *The Story of Elizabethan Drama*. New York: Octagon Books, 1973.

74. Quoted in A. L. Rowse, *The Elizabethan Renaissance: The Cultural Achievement*. New York: Charles Scribner's Sons, 1972.

75. Harrison, *The Story of Elizabethan Drama*.

76. Rowse, *The Elizabethan Renaissance: The Cultural Achievement*.

77. Quoted in Rowse, *The Elizabethan Renaissance: The Cultural Achievement*.

Chapter 8: Literature and the Visual Arts

78. Quoted in Rowse, *The Elizabethan Renaissance: The Cultural Achievement*.

79. Rowse, *The Elizabethan Renaissance: The Cultural Achievement*.

80. Quoted in Byrne, *Elizabethan Life in Town and Country*.

81. Quoted in Byrne, *Elizabethan Life in Town and Country*.

82. Quoted in Rowse, *The Elizabethan Renaissance: The Cultural Achievement*.

83. Quoted in Rowse, *The Elizabethan Renaissance: The Cultural Achievement*.

84. Quoted in Rowse, *The Elizabethan Renaissance: The Cultural Achievement.*

Chapter 9: Science and Superstition

85. Rowse, *The Elizabethan Renaissance: The Cultural Achievement.*

86. Smith, *The Horizon Book of the Elizabethan World.*

87. Quoted in Rowse, *The Elizabethan Renaissance: The Life of the Society.*

88. Quoted in Rowse, *The Elizabethan Renaissance: The Life of the Society.*

89. Rowse, *The Elizabethan Renaissance: The Cultural Achievement.*

90. Quoted in Rowse, *The Elizabethan Renaissance: The Cultural Achievement.*

91. Quoted in Byrne, *Elizabethan Life in Town and Country.*

92. Quoted in Rowse, *The Elizabethan Renaissance: The Cultural Achievement.*

93. Quoted in Rowse, *The Elizabethan Renaissance: The Cultural Achievement.*

94. Rowse, *The Elizabethan Renaissance: The Cultural Achievement.*

95. Quoted in Smith, *The Horizon Book of the Elizabethan World.*

96. Quoted in Rowse, *The Elizabethan Renaissance: The Cultural Achievement.*

97. Quoted in Rowse, *The Elizabethan Renaissance: The Cultural Achievement.*

Chapter 10: Toward the New World

98. Quoted in Smith, *The Horizon Book of the Elizabethan World.*

99. Quoted in A. L. Rowse, *The Expansion of Elizabethan England.* New York: St. Martin's Press, 1955.

100. Rowse, *The Expansion of Elizabethan England.*

101. Quoted in Rowse, *The England of Elizabeth.*

102. Quoted in Jason Hook, *Sir Francis Drake.* New York: The Bookwright Press, 1988.

103. Quoted in Rowse, *The Expansion of Elizabethan England.*

104. Quoted in Rowse, *The Expansion of Elizabethan England.*

105. Quoted in Rowse, *The Expansion of Elizabethan England.*

106. Quoted in Rowse, *The Expansion of Elizabethan England.*

107. Quoted in Rowse, *The Expansion of Elizabethan England.*

108. Quoted in Smith, *The Horizon Book of the Elizabethan World.*

109. Quoted in Smith, *The Horizon Book of the Elizabethan World.*

110. Quoted in Smith, *The Horizon Book of the Elizabethan World.*

111. Smith, *The Horizon Book of the Elizabethan World.*

Epilogue: The Elizabethan Heritage

112. Quoted in S. T. Bindoff, *Tudor England.* Baltimore: Penguin, 1950.

113. Byrne, *Elizabethan Life in Town and Country.*

114. Quoted in Byrne, *Elizabethan Life in Town and Country.*

115. Quoted in Byrne, *Elizabethan Life in Town and Country.*

116. Rowse, *The England of Elizabeth.*

117. Quoted in Rowse, *The England of Elizabeth.*

118. Byrne, *Elizabethan Life in Town and Country.*

119. Rowse, *The England of Elizabeth.*

120. Rowse, *The England of Elizabeth.*

121. Byrne, *Elizabethan Life in Town and Country.*

For Further Reading

Clifford Lindsey Alderman, *The Golden Century: England Under the Tudors*. New York: Julian Messner, 1972. Only about forty pages on Elizabeth, but provides an excellent background to her reign. Good opening chapter on the contributions of the Tudors.

Henrietta Buckmaster, *Walter Raleigh: Man of Two Worlds*. New York: Random House, 1964. Fairly lengthy biography (170 pages) of the poet/adventurer sticks to the facts without attempts at fictional dialogue.

Adéle deLeeuw, *Sir Walter Raleigh*. Champaign, IL: Garrard, 1969. A biography written for younger (elementary-level) readers. Somewhat fictionalized, but hits all the major points. Good use of maps to illustrate sea voyages.

Frank Dwyer, *Henry VIII*. New York: Chelsea House, 1988. One of the *World Leaders Past and Present* series. Nice coverage of all major aspects of Henry VIII's reign. Excellent color illustrations, plus chronology and index. Includes foreward, "On Leadership," by Arthur M. Schlesinger Jr.

Constance Fecher, *The Last Elizabethan: A Portrait of Sir Walter Raleigh*. New York: Farrar, Strauss & Giroux, 1972. Use of dialogue, some fictionalized, makes this biography highly readable. Especially good account of his trial and execution.

Helen Hanff, *Queen of England: The Story of Elizabeth*. Garden City, NY: Doubleday, 1969. Very simply written biography for young readers. No index or bibliography and few illustrations.

Roger Hart, *Battle of the Spanish Armada*. London: Wayland, 1973. Highly detailed yet very readable account of the background, battles, and aftermath of the Spanish Armada. Lavishly illustrated, with good use of maps.

Will Holwood, *Sir Francis Drake*. Chicago: Childrens Press, 1958. This biography of Drake begins with his service under John Hawkins and tells little of his earlier life. Good account of Drake's voyages in the 1570s as well as the defeat of the Spanish Armada.

Edith Thacher Hurd, *The Golden Hind*. New York: Thomas Y. Crowell, 1960. An exciting story, geared to very young readers, about Francis Drake's round-the-world voyage in 1578.

Jean Lee Latham, *Drake: The Man They Called a Pirate*. New York: Harper & Row, 1960. Fairly complete account of Drake's life and adventures. Somewhat fictionalized to make it a more readable story.

Diane Stanley and Peter Vennema, *Good Queen Bess: The Story of Elizabeth I of England*. New York: Four Winds Press, 1990. A good, simply written biography with excellent color illustrations by Diane Stanley.

Ronald Syme, *Walter Raleigh*. New York: William Morrow, 1976. Elementary school–level biography is very short and simple. Black-and-white illustrations. No index.

Dorothy Turner, *Queen Elizabeth I*. New York: The Bookwright Press, 1987. Part of the *Great Lives* series. Definitely for younger readers. Starts with Elizabeth's birth and gives little background. Contains a chapter on contributions of the Elizabethan Era.

Marguerite Vance, *Elizabeth Tudor: Sovereign Lady*. New York: E. P. Dutton, 1954.

Partially fictionalized account of Elizabeth's early life. Gives good picture of how royalty was reared and educated.

Stephen White-Thompson, *Elizabeth I and Tudor England*. New York: The Bookwright Press, 1985. Part of the *Life and Times* series. Excellent overview that deals not only with Elizabeth's life and reign, but also with changes in England, including short chapters on religion, government, and court life. Color illustrations, index, glossary.

Betka Zamoyska, *Queen Elizabeth I*. New York: McGraw-Hill, 1981. Very complete biography on a junior high school level. Includes genealogical chart, chronology, index, and bibliography.

Works Consulted

S. T. Bindoff, *Tudor England*. Baltimore: Penguin, 1950. Part of *The Pelican History of England* series, this volume covers the period from 1485 to 1603. A good, general summary somewhat hampered by the lack of footnotes and a bibliography.

M. St. Clair Byrne, *Elizabethan Life in Town and Country*. London: Methuen, 1961. A close and personal look at the lives of everyday Englishmen, great and small, during Elizabeth's reign. Ample use of contemporary quotations.

David Cecil, *The Cecils of Hatfield House*. Boston: Houghton Mifflin, 1973. Written by a member of the family itself, this traces the Cecils from the time of Lord Burghley to the present. Not an extensive biography of Burghley, but a good portrait.

Edward P. Cheyney, *A Shortened History of England*. Boston: Ginn and Company, 1904. Excellent overview for the reader who wishes a short, understandable account of the basic facts.

A. H. Dodd, *Elizabethan England*. New York: G. P. Putnam's Sons, 1973. Well-illustrated look at the various aspects of life and society in Elizabethan England.

Carolly Erickson, *The First Elizabeth*. New York: Summit, 1983. The author's Ph.D. in medieval history is evident in this scholarly yet entertaining biography of Elizabeth.

Particularly helpful for researchers is the exhaustive index.

————, *Great Harry*. New York: Summit, 1980. Extremely detailed, yet readable, biography of Elizabeth's father. Well researched and documented.

Robert Gray, *A History of London*. New York: Taplinger, 1979. Traces London from its beginnings as a Roman settlement through the 1970s, with attention to physical growth and social and political development.

G. B. Harrison, *Elizabethan Plays and Players*. Ann Arbor: The University of Michigan Press, 1956. History of Elizabethan drama with particular emphasis on actors and the theaters in which they performed.

————, *The Story of Elizabethan Drama*. New York: Octagon, 1973. In this sequel to *Elizabethan Plays and Players*, Harrison discusses how drama developed under various playwrights.

Jason Hook, *Sir Francis Drake*. New York: The Bookwright Press, 1988. Written for young readers, but a good, sprightly summary of Drake's career.

Joel Hurstfield and Alan G. R. Smith, eds., *Elizabethan People: State and Society*. New York: St. Martin's Press, 1972. A wonderful collection of excerpts from letters, speeches, acts of Parliament, and many other documents organized by topic and presenting a good picture of Elizabethan life.

Elizabeth Jenkins, *Elizabeth the Great*. New York: Capricorn, 1967. A highly personal biography of Elizabeth I that goes beyond facts and dates to discuss the queen's personality and its impact on events.

Adrian Morey, *The Catholic Subjects of Elizabeth I*. Totowa, NJ: Rowman and Littlefield, 1978. Very detailed and scholarly examination of the various ways in which the Catholics in England and exiled from England dealt with a Protestant queen.

Fontana Christopher Morris, *The Tudors*. Glasgow, Scotland: Fontana Collins, 1966. More a study of the personalities of the Tudor kings and queens than a history of their reigns. Excellent look at Elizabeth as the woman behind the mask of royalty.

Jasper Ridley, *Henry VIII*. New York: Viking Penguin, 1985. One of the very best and most readable of many biographies of the much-married King of England. Small number of pictures is a bit disappointing.

A. L. Rowse, *The Elizabethan Renaissance: The Cultural Achievement*. New York: Charles Scribner's Sons, 1972. Fourth in the author's series on the England of Elizabeth; this one deals with art, literature, science, and philosophy.

———, *The Elizabethan Renaissance: The Life of the Society*. New York: Charles Scribner's Sons, 1971. Third of Rowse's four volumes on the Elizabethan Era; this one deals principally with social life, including the court, social classes, and leisure activities.

———, *The England of Elizabeth*. New York: Collier, 1950. The first in a series of four books on the Elizabethan Era by one of the most prominent scholars in the field. This volume deals mostly with commerce, government, and religion.

———, *The Expansion of Elizabethan England*. New York: St. Martin's Press, 1955. This volume in the author's series deals not only with overseas expansion, but with relations with Wales, Scotland, and Ireland.

Linda Simon, *Of Virtue Rare*. Boston: Houghton Mifflin, 1982. Biography of the life of Margaret Beaufort, wife of Edmund Tudor and mother of King Henry VII of England. Has good information on the roles of the Tudors during the War of the Roses, although Margaret herself seems to have been rather uninteresting.

Eric N. Simons, *The Reign of Edward IV*. New York: Barnes & Noble, 1966. Comprehensive account of the reign of the great Lancaster king. Excellent source on the War of the Roses.

Lacey Baldwin Smith, *The Horizon Book of the Elizabethan World*. New York: American Heritage, 1967. A comprehensive look, not only at Elizabethan England but also at the rest of Europe and the world beyond. Also contains sections of contemporary works and quotations illustrating various aspects of society. Lavishly illustrated in color.

George M. Trevelyan, *A Shortened History of England*. Harmondsworth, England: Penguin, 1962. Has been called the best single-volume history of England ever written, and with good reason.

Marvelous writer gives all the who's, when's, and where's, along with the how's and why's.

Milton Waldman, *Rod of Iron*. Boston: Houghton Mifflin, 1941. Interesting study of the ways in which power was wielded by English rulers in the sixteenth and first half of the seventeenth centuries. Particular attention paid to Henry VIII, Elizabeth I, and Oliver Cromwell.

Index

Picture Credits

Cover photo by The Bettmann Archive

Ann Ronan Picture Library, 40, 61, 69 (bottom), 77

Archive Photos, 14 (bottom), 25, 60 (both), 83, 98

The Bettmann Archive, 14 (top), 18, 27, 29, 34, 36, 41, 42, 49, 51, 53, 57, 58, 69 (top), 85, 87, 93, 99, 100

Bildarchiv Foto Marburg/Art Resource, NY, 78 (bottom)

Bridgeman/Art Resource, NY, 111

Culver Pictures, Inc., 52, 63, 82, 86

Library of Congress, 13, 43, 92, 112

The Mansell Collection, 17, 23, 74

National Library of Medicine, 95

North Wind Picture Archives, 38, 47, 55, 71, 79

Stock Montage, Inc., 10, 11, 16, 20, 24, 31, 32, 45, 54, 62, 65, 66, 67, 73, 75, 78 (top), 88, 90, 96, 97, 101, 102, 103, 104, 107, 108, 110

The Victoria and Albert Museum, London/Art Resource, NY, 89

About the Author

William W. Lace is a native of Fort Worth, Texas. He holds a bachelor's degree from Texas Christian University, a master's from East Texas State University, and a doctorate from the University of North Texas. After working for newspapers in Baytown, Texas, and Fort Worth, he joined the University of Texas at Arlington as sports information director and later became the director of the news service. He is now vice chancellor for public affairs at Tarrant County Junior College in Fort Worth. He and his wife, Laura, live in Arlington and have two children. Lace's other books include biographies of baseball player Nolan Ryan and artist Michelangelo, and a history of the Hundred Years' War.